THE LONG ROAD HOME

THE LONG ROAD HOME

MARY LYNCH

LONDUBH BOOKS

First published in 2010 by

Londubh Books

18 Casimir Avenue, Harold's Cross, Dublin 6w, Ireland

www.londubh.ie

1 3 5 4 2

Cover by bluett; cover photo courtesy of PJ Lynch

Origination by Londubh Books

Printed in Ireland by ColourBooks, Baldoyle Industrial Estate, Dublin 13

ISBN: 978-1-907535-08-6

*This book is dedicated to anyone who has been wounded,
by whatever means, especially those who have no physical scars.*

Acknowledgements

A special thanks to my two beautiful children, Roisín and Jarlath Geraghty, the loves of my life, who grew up with my past as part of their childhood and to whom I owed a explanation.

Thanks to James and Maureen Lynch, who are the most wonderful parents a soul could wish for, and to my brothers and sisters who have always been there for me in their own unique ways: Seán, Noel, Paddy (PJ), Geraldine, Tom, Peter, Kevin, Lucy, Ruth, Brendan and Gertie.

Thanks to all the people who have helped me to get to where I am. You all know who you are and you are mentioned within these pages of my life. Thanks especially to my friend Anne Nally, who has been on the other end of my phone every day for more than six years now.

I would like to acknowledge the late Gerry Ryan, who encouraged me to speak about my trauma on his radio programme. This gave me the strength to face what I could not face up to before then and the confidence to write my story.

Thanks to my editor, Eileen Bennett, who has had nothing but encouragement for me from the first time I spoke to her and whose wisdom I could not have done without.

Thanks to Morgan Llywelyn, historical novelist, who took precious time to read my story and help it on its journey to publication and to Leo Cooper who introduced me to her.

And finally, thanks to Jo O'Donoghue of Londubh Books, my publisher, who believed in me enough to put her money where her mouth is.

Thank you all from the bottom of my heart.

Lies

Lies,
I hate them,
I lived them,
I lived them to survive,
I lied,
I lied to myself,
The worst lie of all,
So that I wouldn't have to look within,
I lied to everyone,
The lie of society,
Of acceptance.
Forget the lies,
We owe ourselves the truth,
The truth that can only be reached within,
Within our own body, mind and soul,
The wonderful truth of who you really are,
The beautiful truth,
Of what you alone are capable of.
Society will never teach you this,
It teaches you to conform.
Only you can live the truth,
The real truth,
Your truth.

Contents

Prologue

Seek the truth and the truth shall set you free: I have heard this saying all my life but only now do I truly understand it.

I told a lot of lies in my life or withheld the truth. I felt I had no choice but to do this to survive. Growing up in Northern Ireland I withheld the truth. I did not want to burden others with things I had witnessed or experienced and they were doing the same thing themselves.

I went to the USA as an illegal immigrant and was living a lie every day I was there. When I returned home to live in the west of Ireland I withheld the truth of my background because I did not want anyone to judge me or, more importantly, judge my children.

The media in southern Ireland had their own version of the truth and the views of people like me did not even enter their minds. I was guilty by association and so were my children, even though the media had no idea of anything we had lived through.

I was also forced, like so many people, to withhold the truth from myself.

You may well ask how anyone could possibly withhold truth from themselves but we do it all the time in everyday situations. We see something and pretend we didn't because it is too difficult to face. We ignore things that are going on in our lives because if we face them we will have to do something about them. Worse still, we are so traumatised by an event that we completely blank it and pretend it never happened because we are not equipped to deal with it.

I was one of those people who was traumatised. I had to do something to keep the memories at bay so I became a workaholic. It worked until I was so exhausted that I could not use my addiction any longer. I was then given medication to get me through it. This is where the trouble can really start: the medication can replace whatever addiction you already had or it can get you feeling strong enough to go back to the original addiction.

That's what happened to me and I ended up back on medication. I knew enough about addiction to drugs not to want to go there so I was faced with no option but to seek the truth.

What was I running from and what was I hiding?

This did not come in a flash of inspiration. It took years of little memories, which all had to be faced, until I could build a better picture of what really happened to me and why I had been running all my life. When I thought the process was complete I wrote this book for myself to put all the pieces of the jigsaw together and to be honest (which is what I try to be all the time now). I thought that was that and it was over.

A friend suggested I send a couple of chapters to the editor of the local newspaper, who was a complete stranger to me. This I did and she emailed:

> Hi Mary
>
> Read the part of the book you sent me and think it is a fascinating story, I have forwarded it to a publisher to see what they think with a view of having it published. In any event I think it is a story that should be told.
>
> Christina

Before I knew what was happening, I had found somebody to edit the book and that's when one of my greatest fears arose. I emailed her on 31 May 2009:

> Hi Eileen
>
> There are a few things I need to tell you, which you need to know to edit this book and I need to write to release another huge fear in me.
>
> When I met you first and you said that you did not think I would have a problem getting it published. I was delighted but it also created a terrible fear in me.
>
> When you were gone on holidays I had a flashback. It is of a memory I have had all my life but it did not seem to fit in anywhere in this jigsaw so I kept ignoring it.

The memory was of me in the back of a car. I was about eighteen. My friends and I were going out for the night. As we were driving along, there a checkpoint ahead. Nothing unusual about that but I was convinced that it was a Loyalist checkpoint, which may have been common at the time but not in the area I was living.

I was petrified as I had a terrible fear that we were all going to be murdered.

When I had this flashback after meeting you I took it into a meditation. It was only then I realised this was the point when I knew I had to leave the North because if the police sent a loyalist gang in to get me (as they said they would) they would have no choice but to kill everyone who was unlucky enough to be with me. So not only was my family not safe when I was around but neither were my friends.

When I got the email from the publishers two days ago asking for more of the book, I was delighted but it brought this fear up again and I did not sleep well. I cried most of the day yesterday and called a friend and told them that I was terrified that if the book were to be published they would kill me.

Eileen, I know this must sound ridiculous to you but it was as if there were two people in me: a woman of nearly fifty who was delighted that someone might be interested in her story and a terrified eighteen-year-old who was still afraid they were going to kill her.

I could not fully understand this until this morning when I woke up and the fear was still there, rising up from my chest and nearly choking me, In my medi-tation I asked myself: why did I fear them killing me so much as I have no fear of death. I passed that point in that cell they held me in and they knew it.

It was only then that I realised it was not death I feared but *how* they would kill us. They said they would send a Loyalist gang, trained by the Shankill Butchers, to our home, killing everyone there, starting with my mother, if I ever told.

Don't you be worrying about me. I'm off to the

mountains today and will be fine now that I understand this and it will probably help you to understand
things better.

Have a great weekend.

Love and thanks for taking the time to read this

Mary

PS Maybe I'm trying to justify to the eighteen-year-old
in me that I had no option? Maybe I need to justify to
myself today that I had no option? Or maybe I need to
justify to everyone that there was no option that would
not have made things a lot worse than they already
were, even though I think the greatest killer of the soul
is silence.

I now understand something my mother always
says – 'It's a long road that has no turn.' – and maybe I
always knew that some day I would be able to tell this
story without fear of any retaliation and to help others
to understand the consequences of silence.

1

I Had Finally Found
What I Was Looking For

It was the first day of 2009, my fiftieth year. I had driven with my daughter the eighty miles of back roads from the west and crossed the border as it was getting dark.

As I drove with Roisín, who was sleeping like she was un-conscious (she had partied in Galway with her friends the whole night before), the realisation that I was at home filled every cell of my body. The warmth and love that flowed through me was the most wonderful feeling I have ever had.

It was not because I had crossed the border to where I was born, nor even the fact that it was so peaceful in the car listening to Lyric FM. It was because, in my heart, I had found a peace that I knew would travel with me wherever I was to journey for the rest of my time on this earth; a peace that I had been seeking for nearly forty years; a peace that no land, nobody or nothing could give me; a peace that I had finally found in myself.

The plan was for us to meet in our parents' kitchen, north of the border. Who ever could come, we were sure to have a good crowd; after all there were twelve of us, all still alive after the Troubles, and stories to be told from all sides: the activists, the bystanders, the parents, the ex-prisoners and the nurse who had trained in the Royal Hospital in Belfast in the height of the Troubles.

Then there were those of us who had tried to hold our own south of the border, where no one understood the life we had been subjected to, a few miles up the road from the Free State. As children of war we saw things that I prayed my own children would know only from stories told by other people, even if one of those people was their mother.

Roisín woke as the car came to a halt on the front street of my parents' house and asked, 'Are we there yet?'

'Yes,' I replied and smiled as I opened the door of the car and headed for the back door into the kitchen.

This was not the home we were raised in but a modern bungalow the boys had built for our parents twenty years previously. When we got to the kitchen, which as usual was like a sauna, I saw that only Peter had arrived before me.

Dad and Mam were there too: Dad, straight as a die and bright as a button at ninety, had his arms out for the usual hug, which was always a pleasure for me to give.

Mam, who was eighty, hugged us both too as we wished one another a Happy New Year. Peter, my younger brother, had come from Dublin with his partner, Caitriona and young son, Danon.

My youngest sister Gertie arrived in a panic a few minutes later. She had nearly caused an accident on the way.

'What happened?' we asked, as Dad started to make the hot whiskeys.

She had been travelling down the main road and missed her exit. She made a U-turn to go back and heard the sound of screeching brakes. As she pulled in to turn back to see what had happened, a jeep cut her off and two policemen banged on her car window.

The police had never been a welcome sight in our lives as they were usually hammering on our door at five o'clock in the morning. Times had changed but you still did not want to have them banging on your car window on a dark winter's night!

'What the hell are you at?' one of them screamed at her. 'You know there is a jeep-load of policemen in shock down the road!' No more in shock than Gertie, who knew it was entirely her fault but was not about to admit it to these people whom she had first encountered in our home when she was still in the cot.

'Go on and be more careful,' the policeman said, as everyone was okay.

'Well,' said my father, 'Did you tell them where you were going?'

'No,' replied my sister, 'not because they might then know who I was but because I didn't want them to know that I know these roads like the back of my hand.'

Geraldine, the eldest of the girls, was the next to arrive with her daughter Sinéad. Geraldine knew the other side of the war. She worked in the hospital and saw the injuries that were caused by all sides. She never minced her words in saying exactly how she felt about what was going on.

The kitchen door opened and in walked Seán, dressed in a black wool jumper identical to Peter's. Geraldine, always quick with her tongue, could not help but ask if it was Sinn Féin standard issue.

Seán was the eldest of the family and one of the best known. He had been actively involved with the IRA for a long time before he was shot in 1986, with Seamus McElwain. Seamus was not as lucky as Seán and did not survive.

Noel was the next one in from across the road, where he lived alone in the house he had built for himself. Of his five children, four were now adults and out on their own. Gary, his son, had been killed in a motorcycle accident in New York in 2001, at the age of twenty-three.

Ruth, the Sinn Féin Councillor, was next to arrive with her beautiful new baby girl, Teagan, an unexpected bonus born a month before Christmas to the delight of her brother and sister, Piaras and Eimear. The baby smiled to the 'Ooohs' and 'Aaahs' of everyone, especially her two big cousins, Roisín and Sinéad.

The world had hit a major recession, with both sides of the border feeling it. Sterling had hit rock bottom and the shoppers from the South hitting the high streets and supermarkets on the border created an artificial boom for Northern traders. The Southern government was facing one crisis after another after fifteen years of a booming economy.

This was the talk in Dad and Mam's kitchen that night. The recession was going to hit us all but after surviving nearly thirty years of war, this was not life-threatening and we laughed and joked about what we would do to get through it.

Kevin was the next to appear, in from the bottom of the road, where he lived with his wife and five children. He had spent ten of his first thirty years in Crumlin Road Jail and Long Kesh, a casualty of the war, imprisoned first at the age of seventeen.

Brendan, the youngest of the boys, arrived in from Leitrim. He lived there with his wife and three children. Gertie lived close to him (but in County Cavan) with her daughter Sédhna. Gertie and Brendan had never known anything but war as they were brought into the world in the late 1960s.

As Dad continued as bartender, Mam fussed like Father Ted's housekeeper, with a fresh pot of tea and food for all of us as we arrived.

By eleven o'clock all that were coming had appeared, Tom being the last as usual. He came from God-knows-where; he could turn up on your doorstep at any time from anywhere. He drifted as the wind took him, appearing frequently in the townland to visit his two children who lived there with their mother.

Ten of us were there, with no one expecting Lucy to fly in from Florida – she had come four months previously to celebrate Dad's ninetieth birthday and Mam's eightieth – nor Paddy from London, where he had lived on and off all his life.

As the conversation flowed I looked around the kitchen and saw a scene of peace and contentment that I would never have believed possible, even in my wildest dreams.

I drifted off to another time when things were very, very different.

2

LET GO OF THE PAST

The first of us was born in 1954 and over the next fourteen years eleven others followed. There were seven boys and five girls born to my mother and father.

They had both lived in the neighbourhood of Ballagh and the Knocks all their lives. My father was one of five children, my mother was raised with only one brother. Dad's family had been Catholic for generations but my mother's mother had changed religion from Methodist when she married my grandfather in 1922. She took him into her house and land, which was not a popular thing to do at the time.

I was the sixth of the twelve, born in 1959, fourteen months to the day after my brother Tom. Life was fairly hectic in a family of twelve but we were never short of anything or of someone to play with or to talk to. I still remember sunny summers and cold winters with not much happening – or if there was, we were certainly not told about it.

That night in 1972 we were at a play in the local parish hall, which had no heat, and the wind whistled through the cracks in the windows. We stayed warm by laughing and laughing at the local comedian's jokes as he entertained us at the concert.

It wasn't until it was over that he came back out on stage to say that two men had been found murdered on a farm outside Newtownbutler, a few miles up the road. You could have heard a pin drop as everyone wondered who it was. There was a silence in the car coming home that night, a silence I had never experienced in my short life, a silence that I'd never forget as we tried to come to grips with the fact that two of our neighbours had been murdered. One was a cousin of my father's, but more than that, he was one of his best friends.

I have no memory of the funerals, only the talk and the fear that had descended on our little area. I knew there were major problems all over the North at the time, especially in Derry and Belfast, but they were on another planet as far as my young mind was concerned.

This was local: these were our friends, our neighbours and our relatives and there was a fear amongst the adults that seemed unnatural to the mind of a child.

Why were they so afraid? And if they were that frightened we should be terrified. And we were. They did not say anything to us about it because they did not want to worry us, which only served to frighten us more. We heard the whispers. The army did it. They knew the army did it, as any group of locals knows when a murder happens in their patch. Rumours were spread that Michael Naan did it to himself after killing his friend, Andy, but how do you stab yourself with a pitchfork?

Nobody was questioned, nobody charged at that time. The neighbours were supposed to let it go, to forget and get on with their lives, but it had changed how people were. Gone were the simple minds of country folk. The war had now reached our parish and people started to think about how to defend themselves. Some had their first thoughts of retaliation.

Years later, at the time when the Yorkshire Ripper was killing people in the north of England, a plea was broadcast, 'Do you know of anyone capable of these crimes?'

A voice message was left by a man saying that they might be linked to the Fermanagh murders. A month later the office of the *Daily Mirror* in Manchester received a call from the same man who mentioned names. An investigation was launched, a sergeant admitted his involvement and named others.

The staff sergeant was said to have told the detectives, I did the killings, I killed them, Oh my God, yes, I did it. They would not stop screaming. I have been having bloody nightmares about it.

Three soldiers were charged and convicted of these murders. None of them was the Yorkshire Ripper but the murders were just as savage.

Nothing was ever the same again. No one felt safe.

The *Irish Times* reported: 'The murders of two Catholics caused widespread fear in the scattered farmhouses of bitterly divided Fermanagh. The savagery of the killings also aroused particular horror, even though 1972 had already had a shocking toll of violent deaths.'

I think this was when I first started to lie in bed at night and plan how I could save the whole family if the soldiers came to our house. If I stayed awake I could sneak out of our bedroom window down into my parent's bedroom, get my father's gun, load it, go into the kitchen and shoot them. Innocent as I was, I was not so innocent as to think I would be able to kill them all, but I was innocent enough to believe that if I killed one, everyone would know who did it.

A long time afterwards, in a Tai Chi class in Roscommon, the teacher asked everyone individually if they could kill and one by one they replied, 'No.' When he got to me I said, 'Yes.' I knew when I was twelve that I would kill to defend my family, not a thing many twelve-year-olds will ever have to decide, but there was no question in my mind that I would do it.

It was more than a year later that our house was raided for the first time. It was one of the first traumatic things to happen to me.

After those first murders I became adjusted to sleeping light and, as I thought, with one eye open waiting to defend the family when they arrived so I was both surprised and petrified the night the point of a gun woke me.

There in our bedroom, where four of the girls slept, stood three soldiers. One had a gun to my head.

For years afterwards I woke up crying with this vision in my head but only after getting a lot of help could I get past it to what happened next.

We were taken in our bare feet down to the kitchen where the rest of the family was being held. We all stood there for the next few hours as our house and our whole world were ripped apart.

I watched as my father was completely powerless. I was too young to understand that there are times when there is nothing anyone can do. I was to live with this memory for the rest of my life

Many years later I wrote a poem, which I named 'The Floor'.

I do my meditation. It flashes, a floor, a yellow vinyl-tiled floor.
That's it, that's all I can see, a yellow tiled floor.
I cannot lift my head, I'm too afraid.

I know this floor, I know nothing else,
Everything else is strange and foreign to me.
I stare for comfort in the only thing I am familiar with,
The floor.

As we stood there numb to the pain and cold, I watched as men in uniforms speaking with foreign accents ripped our fragile security apart. Local police accompanied them and hurled abuse at us.

A few hours later they were gone but leaving memories I still live with: a shattered home and shattered dreams. They left as they came, without a word about why they were there. That night the war that was outside our door came into our home, a home that was never the same again. The man who was our protector could not protect us from this.

Whenever they returned I learned to be dressed before they reached the bedroom and was never again caught asleep. To this very day I can hear the grass grow as my hearing intensified after that night. I now have to sleep with earplugs to drown out the sounds of everyday life.

After the first time the soldiers usually left with one of my brothers in tow. That first night I built a wall around me to protect myself, a wall that took a few hours to build and over thirty years before I could even begin to dismantle it.

They may have been able to invade our country; they may have had the right to raid our home, but there was one place I knew they could not penetrate and that was the wall that surrounded my body. Neither could anybody else get through this wall, including myself. Until I dismantled it, I could not let go of my past and the burden I carried.

3

Don't Forget to Remember
the Good Times

There was a time when the backs of the ditches were free of British soldiers. We would go off in the morning and not return for hours but we were never alone. There was always someone tailing you and you were always tailing someone else. I tailed Tom because he was older than me and Peter tailed me.

Because there are twelve of us, Peter and I share the position of being the middle children, which apparently is a syndrome now: middle child syndrome. I often wondered is that just Peter and me or all of us between the eldest and the youngest, which would leave ten of us.

Tom and I always seemed to be partners in crime, with Peter trailing behind asking questions. Peter was always asking questions even if he knew the answers. Dad called him Jem after Jem Mohan, a local old man, who was known to have the same ailment.

There were orchards to be robbed in the autumn and nuts to be collected in the glen and plants to eat in the ditches in between. In fact to this day when I am walking in the mountains I know every edible plant and I sample them all. It reminds me of those times of utter freedom when I was a child before the war.

I remember one day that Tom and I decided to rob Eddie Booth's orchard as he had a pear tree and it was the only one in the area. We called him Eddie Bear and, even though I had never seen him, I was well aware of the fact that he was different from us. He was a Protestant; I didn't really know what this meant at the time, only that it was different.

We slipped away from Peter. We knew we might have to make a fast getaway and he was too slow at the time. Off across the fields we went to the lane that led past Lizzy Finney's house to Uncle

Thomas's (our grand-uncle).

Lizzy lived to the left and Eddie to the right of the old lane that was used only by bikes and Eddie's ass and cart. We knew Lizzy well as she would bring us in for tea and Paris buns. I don't think they really came from Paris but they were big and sweet with lumps of sugar on top and we didn't care where they came from. That day we slipped quietly by. We knew we could always get the buns on the way back but we had to get the pears when Eddie had gone to town.

Tom and I checked out the back of the house to make sure the ass and cart were gone. If it was we could be sure Eddie was gone with it as he lived alone.

We were at the top of one of the trees when we spotted Eddie coming in the distance. There was no other sound in the countryside but the birds and the bees and Eddie's ass. We were down and behind the ditch in mighty quick time and were peeking over it when he passed. I looked out in horror.

There he was, just a man. Because I knew he was different I had convinced myself he was a bear, the name we had given him because we couldn't pronounce Booth!

We were luckier than the younger ones like Brendan and Gertie. They did not have that freedom of running through the fields with nothing to fear, free as a bird.

In the autumn going to the glen beside the mid-hill was part of the yearly diary. The hazelnuts were ripe at the end of September. I don't remember ever meeting any of the other local children there or any of them coming with us. When we got there, there was always plenty left for us.

Off we'd go in the morning, nothing with us to collect them in. One of the jumpers would be put on the ground and filled with nuts and tied up to be brought home, where we'd share a few with the wee ones. The big ones were not interested any longer. They were doing what the bigger ones did...

The nuts had to be ripe but apples could be eaten before they were ripe, even though they were bitter and poisonous. The thrill of sneaking out at night and over to the orchard to steal them was worth it. You really had to eat them after going to all that trouble.

At other times we would climb the trees, up the lane from the house, as far up as we could go, with a sharp knife stolen out of the kitchen, and carve our names into the tree. Over the next year we would watch our names swell out as the tree healed its wounds. It was the next best thing to having your name in lights.

Going to the bog was part of the summer diary too. The summers always seemed to be long and hot, maybe because they were the best times. Eating the bilberries as everyone else worked, drinking tea out of jam jars with plenty of milk and sugar, with Mammy's home-made bread (which still tastes as good) thick with butter and covered with jam, was priceless. It always tasted better in the bog, just as it always tastes better in the mountains today, out in the fresh air with no sounds, only the insects humming and a few people talking.

The turf was cut, turned, turned again, stacked and then put in a trailer. Sitting on the top of a full load was the best place to be when it was being brought home. Everything always looked different from a height. When we got the turf home it was thrown into the turf house. There were times when I thought there was more heat produced saving the turf than we ever got from burning it.

Then the hay had to be made and we were the machines at that time. It was cut with the cutting bar, and then it had to be tedded (tossed and turned) until it was dry. You prayed no rain would come or it would have to be done again and again and again. Then the rakes were taken out and the dry hay dragged into rows to be raked in again, this time for the rucks. Your hands by this time would have blisters from dragging the rake through the grass to pick up as much of it as possible, as Dad did not like any left on the ground.

I remember the year my job was working the twister and I felt so important. The twister was a piece of bull wire in the shape of a Z with two pieces of wood on it to protect your hands and a hook at the end. I would catch the hook in the ruck of hay and twist it. The piece of wood closest to the hook would allow the bull wire to move freely through it and the piece in my other hand was stationary. I would twist and twist, fascinated by this simple movement that would make the ropes that would keep the hay from blowing away when the wind came to visit.

We all had our jobs, which changed as we got older. I was about thirteen when I got the best job of all: driving the tractor. Pushing down that big clutch with my short legs was a job in itself but I didn't complain. Daddy would shout, 'Slow down, slow down!' as I revved it and got it to go as fast as possible. When the tractor reached the haggard I reversed it into the hay house and the next two on the assembly line were there to pitch the hay off with forks.

The smell of that hay was sweet and beautiful. Of course the last job could be great craic as you jumped up and down on the fresh hay to flatten it.

At some point the pig had to be killed, which I hated – not that I ever had anything to do with it. This poor little animal had been part of the family for a long time. It was fed mostly boiled potato skins if I remember rightly, but unfortunately the time would come for it to return the favour and feed us for the winter.

Uncle Johnny (Dad's brother) would come, as he was the butcher, and we would go as far away as we could possibly get. The sound of the pig squealing as its throat was cut was nearly enough to put you off bacon for the rest of the year and we did not want that, as it was so good. By the time we got back we hoped that all the blood would be off the back street. I didn't really have a problem with it being cut up, as it no longer looked like the pig. The pieces were salted, put in a tea chest and stored in the corner of the shed.

When the bacon came out, it had to be steeped and boiled before it was fried, to get the salt out. It was still salty but scrumptious with boiled spuds and cabbage from our own garden.

The garden was down the bottom, where I assume the best soil was. Here the cabbage, scallions, onions, lettuce, carrots and potatoes were grown and had to be weeded, which was a back-breaking job even if you were small like me. This field was on the mearning ditch so we could easily make an escape to the neighbours if Dad was not around. Sometimes we'd lie on the bank of the small stream between our land and Tom Grew's and collect water with our jam jars to see who could find the strangest insect that lived there.

When we were thirsty we'd take the scallions and go down to the ram that pumped the coldest, loveliest water to the house. You could put the scallion into the well and drink the water through it; the first straw I had ever seen. At one time we grew carrots for the local market. Not a carrot have I tasted like them since: all you had to do was wring the neck, dust one off and eat it raw.

With the turf in one shed and the hay in another it was time for the apples to be picked off the ground and pitted for the winter to make the tarts. They were sweeter by then but I never remember them being too sweet. When they came out of the pit, the taste had always changed. Later we had blackberries to pick, if they ever got a chance to ripen.

No time for a big garden, Dad always had flowers growing behind a low wall that he built on the back street and on the front ditch, as well as the clematis he grew up the front of the two-storey house we lived in. I remember once waiting all summer long for tomatoes to grow on it and was disappointed when they did not arrive after that beautiful purple flower.

Now with a supply of food, turf and bacon for the winter, all we children had to do was to bring in the turf, milk the cows (not that I ever did this but sometimes I had to get them in the field and bring them back) and try our best to stay warm.

Ours was not a small house but it was small for the lot of us and as we grew it seemed to shrink. We had three bedrooms upstairs after the renovation. Before that I seem to remember going through a trap door, up into a big open space, and with no bathroom to be seen anywhere.

Dad had built a toilet in a wee house away from the main one, a godsend when it was finished. By the time most of us had arrived the renovation had been done and as well as the bedrooms we had the much-needed and welcome bathroom and room for storage upstairs. But it was a cold house, like all houses at the time.

Downstairs were the kitchen (small by today's standards) the hall, the scullery, Dad and Mam's bedroom and the sitting room, which was never used because it was like a fridge.

The kitchen housed the only source of heat in the house. The Rayburn cooker was on 24/7 but, unless you were sitting on top of it, you were cold – so sit on top of it is exactly what we tried to do. The sock press was the little press beside the cooker, where the socks were kept, of course. The hottest place was sitting on top of the sock press but you had two chances of getting there, slim and none. The chair on the other side of the cooker kept only one side of you warm as the other side was exposed to the draughts from the window and two doors which were close by. This room had two windows and four doors and with fourteen people using them to enter and exit it was far from being energy-efficient.

But there was one place that was heaven; the hot press where wee people like me could lie stretched out at night on one of the shelves, looking out through a crack in the door left open just enough to see the TV. You had a roasting hot cylinder underneath you with no lagging jacket to stop the heat from rising between the open lath shelves.

That TV, even though it was the one of the first in the county, rented from the electrical shop in town, was a long-awaited arrival. I was so excited the day it appeared that I went into the sitting room and burned that many papers to try and warm the room that I set the chimney on fire.

This was the life I was brought up in. This was the home that was invaded in my fifteenth year by men in uniforms, carrying guns that shattered my dreams of peace and my peaceful dreams.

Three years later they took me into a barracks (I don't know where) and left me so emotionally scarred that it took me more than thirty years to remember.

I was left with no choice but to leave the place I was born into, trusting no one, not even my own family – and sometimes not even myself. These early childhood memories were all I had to hang on to when I had to face brutal memories in order for my healing to take place.

4

Work: the Acceptable Addiction

Children instinctively know what to do to survive and I was no exception. I realised very quickly that if I put my mind to something else I could forget what I could not face.

As the Troubles continued we adjusted into as normal an existence as we could, just to survive.

I left primary school, barely able to read and write, and headed into the brand-new secondary school. This school was built for us Catholics so that we would not have to share the local High School with the Protestants. Our church segregated us so that we would not be contaminated by the heathen ways of our neighbours!

I came to love this school because I loved to learn and, with teachers interested in our future, I thrived. Even though English was not my best subject and was the only exam I ever failed, I always loved to write and I wrote my first poem, called 'Spring', when I was about eleven.

> *Spring is the time for budding trees,*
> *The sun comes out and we have a breeze,*
> *The daffodils and all the beautiful flowers,*
> *All come out, in the spring's long hours.*
> *The baby animals are born in spring*
> *And the birds come back to sing,*
> *The grass is getting a dark, dark green*
> *And the countryside is beautiful to be seen.*

Over the next few years, the home that had protected us from the war became part of it.

I worked hard at school. It occupied my mind and when I did my exams I did better than I expected. I loved that time in school and university beckoned, but not for me. I wanted to be a nurse: it was all I ever wanted to be. Geraldine, my older sister, had finished school two years before me and started to work in a factory in the town, which really annoyed Mammy. She eventually convinced her to try nursing (Mam can be very persuasive when she needs to be) so Geraldine was off to Belfast to train in the Royal Victoria Hospital.

The agreement was that she would try it and if she didn't like she would come back home. She liked it and stayed, which should have made things easier for me when I went for my interview in the same hospital, but it didn't. It was not to be.

I remember the interview well and the nurse in the royal-blue uniform saying to me, 'You only want to be a nurse because your sister's a nurse.'

I was so shy. I wanted to say, 'I have always wanted to be a nurse,' and even to say that my sister had to be bribed to go into nursing, but I didn't and I did not get in.

I could have followed my friends to university but I reckoned if they all got teaching (that was what most of them went for) there would be too many teachers. Anyway, deep down, I knew it was not the road for me.

I thought, 'If I can't do nursing, I will travel,' but you needed money to do that so I got a job in Wellworth's shop in Enniskillen, which I can honestly say was the most boring time of my life. It did not suit me to be pinned in behind those little boxes of counters with all the merchandise around me to serve the customers.

If this was not bad enough, the cold wind that blew in through the door at the top of High Street would skin you if you were unlucky enough to be on any counter near it. It was worse if you were on the vegetable counter, which is where I was a lot of the time.

Six months later I saw an advertisement in the paper for a job as receptionist in a local hotel and I applied and got it. I thought, 'Well, at least it will be warmer.' It was and I loved it. There was always a buzz. They sent me on a training course in Portrush Hotel and Catering College, so for the next year I was up and down from the North Antrim coast, where I met friends I still have.

Everything was going great until that night over Christmas in 1977 when the hotel was bombed.

It was a quiet evening and I had changed shifts with one of the other receptionists. She came in to have a chat with me as she was out with friends and when the phone rang she answered it.

'There's a bomb in the hotel,' she said. Always great in a crisis, I called the manager, who was at home, and proceeded to get everyone out. This wasn't difficult as they were not many about. I do recall a German guest did not want to leave but we eventually persuaded him.

Later after the police had arrived, the bomb went off. It caused damage to a few of the bedrooms in the new wing where it had been planted.

Naturally, as I was the person to book in the man who planted the bomb, I was questioned.

I told them what happened. A room was booked and when the guest arrived alone I called Tommy the porter to bring up his bag. Tommy could not be found so I offered to bring up the bag myself, as we were not very busy. He declined and went to his room and that was the last I saw of him. But it was not the last I saw of the police. I was taken from the hotel the next day to be interviewed again.

I always knew something happened that day that changed me for ever but it was not until thirty years later that I was strong enough to face it and even then I found it to be the most difficult thing I had to do in my whole life.

Within months I left that hotel. I had now finished my exams and had the training to get a job anywhere in the country as a receptionist. I chose Dublin and hitched there one day for four job interviews. I was offered three jobs and took the one closest to the city centre because it had the easiest access both to my brother and to the road home. But I could not settle, a trait that was to become a constant in my life. I could not pinpoint what was wrong but I was not happy and immediately began trying to persuade different friends to come away with me. We chose Germany because one of the girls had an uncle in Münster but one by one the other girls dropped out until my only option was to go alone or not go at all, which I never even considered.

It was Easter 1979. I was now nineteen years old and when I told Mammy I was going to Germany she laughed. She did not believe me. She and Dad were going to Galway to visit my uncle for the weekend, which was a rare treat for them and I was minding the wee ones. On the Sunday night I went out the road to where my brother lived with his wife and children. 'Can you bring me to Maguiresbridge in the morning?' I asked.

'No problem,' he said. 'Be here at half past eight.'

Next morning, on the way to Maguiresbridge, he asked where I was going.

'West Germany,' I replied and he laughed.

'See you tonight,' he said as I got out of his car.

'See you in September,' I answered.

Left alone on that spring morning I nearly balked as the cars flew by me. I looked to the heavens and said, 'I know I have to get out of here. If I am on the right road show me a sign.'

I was always a great believer in signs.

Not two minutes later a lorry pulled up beside me and as I climbed in I asked, 'Where are you going?'

'A lot further than you,' he replied.

'I doubt that,' I said, 'I'm going to West Germany.'

'I'm going to Scotland,' he said 'but I'll get you a lift on down to London with someone I know,' and he did.

Early next morning after a few hours' sleep as his friend drove thought the night, I arrived in London. From there I caught a train to Dover and a boat to Ostende in Belgium.

I had no fear; it was as if I did not care what happened to me, I just had to get away.

I sent a postcard to my mother from Belgium but found out later that it took weeks to arrive. By this time she was frantic and thought I was lost for ever. There was no e-mail, no mobile phones or such paraphernalia at that time, not even a phone – just the unreliable postal service.

From Ostende I took a train to Münster, where a neighbour of my mother lived, but he was not expecting me. His niece, my friend, had written to him at some time to say we might be over but she had backed out.

The train reached the city at one in the morning and I was the only person to get off. I spoke no German and had no German money but knew from a friend that one of our coins was the size of a German mark and could be used in the phone.

So off I went to find a phone. I had the man's number, which I hoped would be the right one.

I rang it, he answered and I explained who I was. 'Stay where you are,' he said, 'don't move. I'm on my way.'

He picked me up that night and I slept like a baby when he put me in the spare room.

I was free of it all – or so I thought.

Next morning he brought me to a hotel on the outskirts of the city and got me a job as a chambermaid. I would have a place to stay in the staff quarters.

'Call me if you need anything,' he said, as he drove off.

'I'll be fine,' I said.

I had no intention of calling him unless I really needed him. I was grateful for his help in getting me this far.

When I lay that night in the twin-bedded staff room I was to share for the next five months with a nice but snooty young German girl, I think it was then that I first had time to realise what I had done.

Not that I had any feeling of regrets – it was the reality of the situation that hit me as I lay there and heard all the students and workers pass by speaking a foreign language.

'Christ,' I thought, 'what if no one speaks English?'

When my roommate appeared she was not much help as she spoke in German even though I later found out she had good English.

Next morning I faced a staffroom of different nationalities as I tried to negotiate my way around a buffet table of food, the likes of which I had never seen before.

I thought the bread looked vaguely familiar and I was sure the cheese couldn't be that different. It was but I ate it anyway. I drank water with it to take the cramps of hunger from my stomach but they could not take the fear from my gut.

Off I went with two Portuguese women who tried to teach me German as we cleaned toilets, hoovered rooms and changed beds over the next few months.

Maria spent most of the time laughing as I tried to speak what sounded to me like bad English. I had never heard German being spoken before but it was odd to call my mother and father *meine mutter* and *mein vater*.

Confused is the only way I could describe how I felt when in the morning one person would say, 'Guten Morgen' and the next person said, 'Guten Tag' – that is how little I knew.

But I got by. I began work at five every morning, starting in the leisure centre, something that was unheard of at the time in Ireland, either north or south of the border. In the north the hotels had come to resemble the barracks with all the security.

Five in the morning was not an unusual time for me to be up as it was around the time the army and police would come.

I remember my boss so well; she was tall and stick-thin and wore a pencil skirt. She reminded me of my domestic science teacher, Mrs Brown, for several reasons; tall, thin, pencil skirt and would let you off with nothing.

Once she called me from the fifth floor of this Grade A hotel to the basement to point out a tiny piece of paper I had missed. Not a woman of many words, she just pointed. I understood and it never happened again.

I learned that day that sign language is truly an international language!

Of the Germans I can say that they sure taught me to work. Foreigners did all the cleaning and those German hotels were impeccable. I never had a problem working hard after that. My mother had always said I would make a better supervisor than a worker as I got off with so little work as a child. Geraldine was two years older and did all the inside work with Mam and there were plenty of boys to help Dad so I think I slipped the through the net then but was to make up for it later in life.

Later in New York I had two jobs at times and ran a business from the bedroom of our apartment. We slept in the corner of the room. Later in Roscommon my neighbour would say I was the best worker in the town. He said it as if I should be proud of this addiction, this socially-accepted addiction that is held in high esteem while it destroys lives, the lives of the person suffering from it and the family around them.

I had learned by this time that when working hard I could temporarily forget. It was like a drug that would ease the pain of memories, a drug that I would continue to use and abuse for the next twenty years until I was so exhausted from it that I had no choice but to face the past of brutal memories or a future of prescription drugs.

5

Wherever I Ran,
I Ran Right Back to My Problems

Life in Germany was so different; no British soldiers or police on the streets, no news reports about the Troubles, even if I could understand what they were saying. I was safe, I was free and nobody seemed to know or care about the situation in the North of Ireland. The only thing in Ireland that the Germans knew about at that time was the Dubliners.

I had been there a few weeks and made friends, young Germans and French women and men who found me a great asset to their English language studies as they trained in hotel management at the hotel.

Uwe was a tall, gangly young German boy who was a waiter and mad to better his English. He realised that I was lonely and knew that I would love to speak to someone who was fluent in English. I had by this time pains in my jaws trying to get around those strange words! When he said he would bring me to friends of his who spoke English I was delighted so off we went down the path by the river into the town. You can imagine my surprise when he brought me to a British Army mess. I was speechless; I can honestly say it was one of the very few moments in my life when I was afflicted by this condition.

I certainly wasn't at liberty to run. I was not about to make any sudden moves so I walked after him up to the bar, my mind racing. What am I going to do? How the hell can I get out of here as fast as possible?

The large square room was bare, with only a few soldiers at a table playing cards and one at the bar drinking.

I thought, 'I can handle this,' but I really did not have a choice.

At this point Uwe had no idea what was going on in my head.

He proceeded to the bar and introduced me to the lone, slightly intoxicated soldier there and was even excited as he explained that I was from Northern Ireland.

The soldier, having just got back from a tour of duty there, spat venom at me. I returned it – to the shock of both my German friend and myself, as any fear about where I was left my body. I did not care. I had met one of those people who had terrorised my childhood and I had no intentions of letting the opportunity go as I might never get one again. Minutes later I turned on my heel and left a lot faster than I had come in, as the realisation of where I was hit before anyone had a chance to recover from what I had just said. Uwe was hot on my heels.

Well, as my mother would say, 'That put paid to that.'

Uwe was not satisfied. How he convinced me to visit an English couple's home I'll never know but the next Sunday we were off again into the town. This time I met Doc and Margaret.

Doc, it transpired, was also in the British Army and about to retire. I could never visualise him in a uniform, maybe because I thought of all soldiers as being young. Doc a was lovely gentleman and Margaret was a real lady and I must say I spent some lovely times in their company. But I found it was a friendship I could not continue when I returned home to the reality of our differences.

The weeks moved quickly into months and it was getting time to move. Mam and I had planned a trip to see Dad's sister in Connecticut. Dad wouldn't come because he did not like flying.

By this time I had made lots of friends and shared my twentieth birthday with a Spanish boy and a German girl. We had a party down by the lake, which was beside the hotel. We celebrated with all our friends.

We made lots of promises about staying in touch as I headed back on the journey I had travelled five months earlier.

This time I planned a stop in London to see my brother Tom, who was as mad as a hatter. When I got to his flat he decided to bring me to a pub where a few local people from home hung out. As I got on the back of his motorbike my memories of how he would rally round the roads at home came back. He would nearly scrape my ankle as he went around the corners. 'He's older now,' I thought logically, 'it will be grand.'

How wrong I was!

'He must be colour-blind!' I thought, as we flew through red traffic lights. I vowed I would walk back; I had no intention of getting up on that bike behind him again.

After a good night out, when it was time to go home I refused point-blank to get back on a bike but Tom convinced me to go with Barry, a neighbour from home.

Standing my ground, I said I would, but not without a helmet. We borrowed a helmet from an elderly man at the bar. Elderly to us! He was probably around forty but that was twice my age at the time.

Off we went but we had only got around the first corner when Barry hit a car head-on and I was flung over the car and slid down the road.

With a helmet split in two beside me and the jeans ripped off one leg I lay there, coming in and out of consciousness. I remember someone saying, 'Is she dead?' before the ambulance arrived.

With broken bones in my hand and the skin ripped off my left leg I was discharged from hospital. I crawled back up on the back of Tom's bike in the middle of the night with his promise that he would not pass thirty miles an hour. He didn't.

Waking up the next morning with pains in places that I didn't know I had places I abandoned all notions I had of hitching and took a taxi to the airport.

Someone had called Barry's father as he had one of the few phones in the area and Dad and Noel came to Belfast to meet me. Dad was standing with his arms out and it was one of the first big hugs I ever remember getting from him.

It was great to be home. Things have got to have changed, I thought, but my short stint of peace was soon broken by the bangs on the door at five the next morning. I had been used to this but now I had to get used to it all over again and I was sickened. When they searched the middle room where I was sleeping, they found all the maps and postcards I had brought home with me from Münster. They were not that important in the usual scheme of things but the IRA had injured four British army bandsmen in a bombing in the centre of Brussels that day. As the soldier ran down the stairs with the maps, he was ecstatic

'For God's sake,' said Paddy, my brother, 'Mary was working out there.' We were now so used to them searching our house that we gave them backchat. It was our house after all, wasn't it?

There was nothing more about it. He had thought I was over there checking the place out, I laughed at the idea of it.

Shortly afterwards the IRA did bomb the British Army barracks there. Christ, I thought, I can go nowhere.

Mam and I went to the States in September for three weeks in another alien culture but it was a rest that we both needed. I ripped the bandages from my hand and dived into my aunt's swimming pool that lay invitingly at the back of her house.

Connecticut is beautiful and in the fall even more so and we had a wonderful time there. This way of life was not unlike that of Germany and a place Ireland headed rapidly into in the years to come. It was a materialistic society and even if I was impressed by the scenery it was not a way of life I was used to or indeed impressed by. I talked about coming back to New York but my Aunt tried to explain that they were in the middle of a recession and there was no work.

When we returned home I signed on the dole for the first and only time in my life. Someone told me that if you got a job south of the border and came off the dole in the north you would get a disturbance allowance, so that's what I did.

Eighteen pounds a week for six months gave me a chance to decide what my next move would be. I needed this allowance as the pay for my receptionist's job in Navan wasn't much to write home about. I stayed there for the six months, spending my free time hitching either home or up to my sister Geraldine in Belfast.

Geraldine was a qualified nurse now and lived in Belfast with her friends, a mixture of Catholics and Protestants and I always had great craic there. As nothing in the line of entertainment was available in Belfast at that time we would end up at house parties all over the place.

Six months later the disturbance allowance was finished. It was time to move so I decided to head back to the States with a cousin.

It was not that I was overly impressed with America but staying in the North or anywhere on the island of Ireland for that matter was not an option and even though I had family in England, it was never a runner for me. It never crossed my mind for a second to go there: I had enough of them in uniforms in our house and on our roads and I had no intentions of ever living amongst them.

So back across the Atlantic I went, this time to the Bronx, New York. I stayed for a few weeks with a cousin and then moved in with a nurse from Roscommon who had advertised for someone to share her apartment. Ann and I got on pretty well but she was much older than me. She worked in the VA hospital, dispensing methadone to soldiers of another war.

I joined an Irish-run nursing agency and worked anywhere and everywhere they sent me. I knew nobody in the neighbourhood, so it suited me to lie low on Kingsbridge Road.

I had to get used to the New York cops. I remember how scared I was when I first saw them on the streets but I soon learned to lose that fear. The subways were not the safest places to be but I felt safer there than I had at home and would travel them day and night at all hours. I never once had a problem on them but must say when the red berets first came on they were a welcome sight. These were volunteers, mostly experts in martial arts, who would travel the subways at night to protect the passengers, but then everyone started to wear the same berets and we were left confused as to who we could trust.

As I was travelling on a train one night (or should I say early one morning) a young man came over and asked if I was Irish. We were never hard to identify, as most of us were a lighter shade of pale.

I think I am a pretty good judge of character so I chatted away to him and when we got to my stop he said, 'I'll walk you home. You should not be walking alone at this time of night.'

I felt like saying that I might be safer walking alone because I had no idea who he was but home was down a main street so I agreed. His name was Kevin Monaghan. He worked in media for NBC Sports and he had a huge interest in the Troubles as he was Irish-American. I found out later that he had worked on a project in Northern Ireland in the summer of 1977 when we was a student. He walked me home and asked me out. We went out a few times but remained friends for longer. I remember he would continually ask me questions about the North. All I wanted to do was cry but I didn't. He kept saying, 'You are a survivor, Mary.' I never knew what he meant. What else could I do but try and survive as best I could.

I also got to know his flatmate, Shay Kelly from Dublin. Shay and I got on great. He used to look out for me. I think he was older than Kevin and me. We understood things that Kevin could not get his head around as he was born and raised on a different planet from us.

Shay moved on to London but kept in contact with me for a while. I think deep down he knew I was a troubled soul and he recognised himself in me. Later, after the hunger strikes, I was back in New York trying to make it my home while I decided where to go next. A group of people called the Irish-American Caucus was holding a symposium on the Troubles to get attention in the media. I had met a woman from Donegal at the demonstration outside the United Nations building and she asked me to draw some pictures for it. I have no idea why I drew pictures of people being tortured but that's what I did – large pictures drawn with charcoal, horrible pictures. I felt so cleansed afterwards.

There were a lot of reporters at the symposium as Seán McBride was speaking. He was the son of Maud Gonne and had been Chief of Staff of the IRA in the 1930s.

A week later I had a letter from Shay with a clipping out of the *Guardian* newspaper in London written by a journalist who had attended. He called it 'An Irish Wake in New York'. He wrote: 'The only good thing about the symposium were the pictures drawn by Mary Lynch,' – and he compared them to Goya. I had no idea who Goya was and never asked. A long time afterwards, when I was in Lanzarote with my sister Geraldine, we were in the home of an artist and the guide mentioned the name Goya. I told Geraldine this story.

'Do you not know who he was?' she said.

'No,' I replied.

'He was a Spanish artist and he painted a lot of pictures of war.'

I don't think my pictures were that great. I think what the journalist recognised was raw emotion drawn.

Years later I was listening to Pat Kenny talking to an American reporter about the OJ Simpson trial. It was Kevin Monaghan and I thought, 'Isn't it a small world!'

One morning as I finished a night shift as a nurse's aid a young woman came in to replace me. 'Where are you from?' she asked.

'Ireland,' I replied, too tired even to notice her Northern accent.

I had now been more than six months in the country and had met no young Irish. This was 1980 and the influx of Irish had not begun.

'Which county?' she laughed.

'Oh. Fermanagh.'

Nuala was from Tyrone. She was about to go home on holidays but before she did she introduced me to her brother Fay (Phelim) Devlin and his two friends, Nashi (Ignatius) and Plunkett.

They lived just around the corner and we became great friends: well, we did our share of fighting but they were a good substitute for my brothers and I never had any problems with having male friends, probably because I was reared with so many boys.

It was Plunkett who told me on the street one day that my brother, Kevin, had got sixteen years in Long Kesh. He assumed I knew but we still had no phone at home. Plunkett had heard from his brother the night before.

Nuala, Fay and the boys were from Pomeroy. A few years later, when the young Irish were flooding into New York, I wrote to Kevin: 'You know, Kevin, half of Pomeroy must be in New York!'

In his reply he said, 'Well, Mary, if they are, the other half are here in Long Kesh!'

I remember sitting in the window of my apartment crying about my brother Kevin and feeling so guilty that I had left Northern Ireland. But I did not want to go back there.

I continued to work all the hours God sent and when Christmas came eleven months later and I had still not bonded with the city I decided to pack all bags and return home for good.

I was never a lover of New York but looking back I now realise New York was not the problem. I did not feel at home anywhere, I had no home. Before I left I wrote a poem to try and explain to my friend Kevin Monaghan and myself why I needed to go home and how I felt about that leave-taking.

Leaving America

I wish I could sit down and tell you why, it's so hard for me to say goodbye,
If I could, maybe then you would understand how it feels to be,
A victim of something understood less by you than me,
I could sit and talk all night but you would still be very far out of sight,
You never lived in Northern Ireland so I can't expect you to see

What living in your country really meant to me.
You see I love my freedom, just like you,
But what is freedom to me without my family to share in it too.
All we asked for is what you call 'human rights',
So it was only a matter of time before people stopped marching
    and started to fight.
So can you really call it a crime, to fight for something that is
    rightfully thine.
But can I really expect you to see?
No, you were born in the land of freedom, not me.

With bags and baggage in tow I went home but after two raids in ten days I had my bags packed again and was on my way back to the Big Apple. I decided that if I could not live in Northern Ireland, the next best thing I could do was to make it possible for the family to come to me.

Over the next five years a lot of them did come and I kept them in my apartment and found them jobs and apartments of their own to move on to. Lucy was the first to arrive, then Tom and his wife Chrissie, followed by Peter and his wife Marie and daughter Joanne. Ruth and her partner Noel arrived later.

Kevin went to New York with his wife Loretta when they were forced to leave Dublin after receiving a lot of hassle from the security forces there. Loretta was asked to clear her desk in Aer Lingus a few weeks after she started working there for 'security reasons', even though she had spent the previous three years in Belfast working for British Airways without a problem. She was not married at the time and was never convicted of or involved in anything. Kevin and Loretta returned home the day of the Good Friday Agreement in 1998 to raise their children in the North, beside where they were both born.

By the time I left they were all settled and continued to do as I had. Over the next twenty years this city that never sleeps fed, clothed and comforted eight of my immediate family, with their partners, in our years of exile. All the family except Seán spent time there, including my parents.

Two of us married there, four of my nephews and nieces were born there to three different families and Gary, my eldest nephew, was killed there.

To this day if I watch any programme on TV that shows those streets I have nothing but good memories of my home from home, even though I found it hard to settle there or anywhere else for a very long time.

I remember the flight back after my brief visit home so well. We were in the air for more than ten hours and could not land at Kennedy because of the snow. I was in a panic because I knew I was not going back to Ireland. I would have to make some kind of life for myself somewhere in America. Now that I had made the decision I was afraid I might not get in so it was a long wait as we circled the runway.

When I got to immigration I was so fed up that when I was asked, 'Do you intend to work here?' I found I could easily reply, 'I have no intentions of working here,' and the official believed me.

I was like a scalded cat as I ran through that airport, afraid that someone might follow me and send me home again. I got to the taxi rank where there was about a foot of snow and no one would take me to the Bronx so I had to settle for midtown Manhattan. It cost me $100, which was a fortune at the time, but I didn't care. I just wanted to get out of that airport. I had gone back to Northern Ireland so many times and nothing had changed. I had a terrible fear of being anywhere near the police or the army.

This time I moved in with my cousin John and his lovely wife Mary from Mayo. It was great; she fed me as if there was a famine coming. I continued to work for the agency and when the hunger strikes started in Long Kesh, I ventured downtown to meetings and demonstrations outside the British Consulate in Manhattan. Maybe there was nothing I could do but I needed to be with my own people. Not that there were many of us but enough to have the Press interview us. When I was asked questions I could say nothing, only cry.

I wrote poems that spewed anger and bitterness and left New York for Los Angeles the day Bobby Sands died on hunger strike.

I wrote this poem on 10 September 1981.

> *Bobby, you died of hunger and pain and still people ask, 'Was this man insane?'*
> *I guess they could not imagine with your life you would pay,*
> *For your freedom and that of your country some day.*

But then after you came our brave Francis Hughes,
Followed by eight more courageous men
And more will die; as Britain tries to tell the world you are
    criminals,
Not freedom-fighting woman and men.
You asked us to imagine what you went through,
What one-day in H-Block really did to you,
But you knew our minds could never conceive
The hurt and humiliation you went through for what you
    believed.
I know freedom is what you have now,
I know you are happy somewhere, somehow.
For the pain and anger you went through have to have a reward
    somewhere for you.
You know God sent his only son to this earth and he died for us
    thirty-three years after birth,
But, Bobby, you too died to set us free so that one day we would
    have our liberty.

I was on the run again as I could not bear it. I stayed in LA with a friend of Ann's (the nurse I had lived with). One day I fell asleep from exhaustion on Malibu Beach and woke up with my legs swollen and burned.

From LA I headed to Phoenix, Arizona, to track down cousins Dad had there. I remember phoning Tommy and telling him what plane I would be arriving on. 'I will be carrying a rucksack and have a big straw hat on me.'

He told me later he was puzzled when he came to the airport to pick me up as he had no idea who I was and if I was twenty or sixty. 'How much did it cost you to fly down?' he asked, as we left the airport.

When I told him he replied, 'Did you fly on the wing?' Tommy was a very funny man.

That first night I arrived, he saw the state of my burned legs. He walked out into the garden and cut a piece of an aloe vera plant, which I rubbed on my legs. They were so much better by morning. I was impressed. This part of the States was like another planet compared to New York.

I stayed with Tommy and his wife Lucy for a few weeks. I found my six second cousins there and had a good time but even there, ten thousands miles from Long Kesh, all the news was about the hunger strikes and everyone wanted me to explain what was going on.

How was I supposed to explain why men had to do this to get their basic human rights as prisoners of war?

From Arizona I headed back to California, this time to San Francisco, and stayed with an Irish-American girl, Maureen Murphy, who is still a friend. She was at demonstrations there and I was back on the street as the hunger strikers continued to die. From there I went up to Sacramento in Northern California, where I traced more of my father's relatives before heading back to New York.

By this time the latest prisoner to go on hunger strike was Kevin Lynch and our newfound cousins in Arizona and California were frantic trying to find me to in order for me to convince them that this was not my brother. Kevin was still on remand in Crumlin Road Jail at this time.

Back in New York I had to make a decision. Was it time to move on? It was 1981 and the young Irish were starting to flood into the city as the recession at home drove them out. My sister Lucy was on her way out to me and I had to stay until she got settled but I thought of maybe going to another part of the States.

It was not work or money I was in search of but of peace, which did not seem to be anywhere I went.

I always felt lost, as if I belonged nowhere.

That is what I was to learn later in life – you can't run from the problem. It follows you wherever you go as it did me for years until I was forced to face it: forced on to my hands and knees in my kitchen in a town in the west of Ireland where I had everything that a normal person would have been happy with.

But I was not normal, I was suffering from post-traumatic stress and by then I had no choice but to face it. I was cornered and I had no place else to run and I was too exhausted from work to hide behind that any longer.

6

LET GO AND TRUST

Lucy arrived in New York at the age of eighteen. She was hard to handle. It was her first time away from home and she treated New York as if it was a small town in Fermanagh. For the first time in a long time I had responsibility for another person and I didn't like it. When she was there only a few weeks and hadn't yet lost the run of herself and while I was still deciding when I would move on, we went out with a friend one night for a few drinks to Durty Nelly's on Kingsbridge Road.

I wanted to go on from there to the Archway Bar to see a band I'd seen in the Catskills the week before. Lucy wanted to go home but I dragged her with me and went to the toilet while she got us drinks.

He told me later that he spoke to me as I passed him but I was too mad with Lucy to hear anything. As I made my way back a man's voice said, 'Don't I know you?'

Well I was not in the humour for any chat-up line like this but when I looked up to answer I looked into the eyes of a man I knew I would like. I just knew.

'I don't think so,' I replied and he asked me where I was from. We started to talk about people we both knew. Before I knew what I was doing I was up on a stool beside him, chatting away. Lucy came up with my drink, said, 'I'm going home,' and left.

He introduced himself as Martin but I automatically started to call him Marty and he never contradicted me even though nobody had ever called him that before. It was weeks later after I had got used to it that he explained this to me.

Marty and I started going out together and I abandoned all plans to move. Two years later we married in New York City. We both worked hard and saved just as hard and in 1985 I convinced him it was time to go home, I don't know if he was ready but I could

not stay another minute in the Big Apple. Marty had decided that
if he was going back he was going back to farming so we started
negotiating to buy the family farm from his mother. This meant
we would be living in the west of Ireland, where he was from, and
not the North, which suited me. I wanted to get back to Ireland, but
south of the border.

My time with my boss Lorna was over as she was winding down
her business. I first met Lorna when my friend Nuala called and
asked if I would go to Florida to mind an elderly lady for the winter.
I had very little work at the time and Marty and his friends were
going to California so I met Lorna in an apartment in Central Park
West. She hired me to look after her mother, Mae, and we flew to
Florida the next day. Lorna had an apartment in Palm Beach where
Mae spent the winters. Palm Beach was where the rich and famous
went to rest and retire.

The apartment had a balcony overlooking the ocean in one of
the best areas of the island. I had a car to drive, a charge account
in all the local shops and also in the Breakers Hotel. This hotel we
went to most nights and was one of the most exclusive in the States
at the time.

It was beautiful but Mae had Alzheimer's and could be very
difficult to handle. Eating out was not always the most pleasant
experience.

When the winter was over and they were heading back to
New York, Lorna asked me if I would work for her in her office. I
didn't want to tell her I was illegal so to put her off I told her that
I had a contract with the nursing agency and couldn't leave. But
she persisted. She knew my predicament quite well but never said
anything.

One day she came to me and said she had bought a company
in Florida in my name so I could work under that company name,
which I did for the next few years. Lorna was a lonely woman. Her
husband was a rich Texan who had made his money in oil. He
rarely came to New York and she trusted no one but I knew she
trusted me.

When I got married it was on a Saturday. I worked for her on
the Friday and was back in the office on the Monday. It was her way
of checking if my loyalty still lay with her. She once said to me, 'You
may not have book knowledge, Mary, but you are streetwise.' How

right she was – but she never knew why I had to be.

My sister-in-law worked for her too, as did some of my friends. If the cat had to go to the hospital, I brought it there. If Mae needed something I made sure she got it. Nothing to do with my job but I did as she asked.

What I did most of the time was to rent out Lorna's apartments. She owned two brownstones between Madison and Park, one on 73rd Street, one on 67th, and two buildings on the corner of 62nd and Lexington Avenue. These are all prime locations in Manhattan.

We also rented apartments in other prime locations, furnished them and sublet them. A chauffeur drove me around Manhattan in a limousine. For all this strenuous work I was paid extremely well, with a bonus every time I rented an apartment. They were rented to the rich and famous. The Rolling Stones' manager had a office in one of the buildings, where Mick Jagger's artwork hung on the walls. Mick's first wife, Bianca, lived in one of the brownstones. I remember renting to Peter O'Toole's ex-wife in Greenwich Village. You never knew who you would meet and we met a lot of interesting people.

Once I rented the ground-floor apartment on 73rd to a writer called Roger Rosenblatt, who was writing a book called *Children of War*. I talked to him a few times as he renewed his lease and when he left he give me a copy of his book. I remember reading the beginning of it, where he wrote about children in Belfast. I could read no more because I was aware that these children included me, but I did not feel that people like me had any right to talk about it. We did not come from the heart of it, the cities, but from the fringes, the border.

Lorna and I understood each other and worked very well together until she no longer needed me and I was ready to go home. Funny how everything comes to a natural ending if we allow it. I have found since that every time I do this I have only good memories of those times, which is the case with Lorna and Mae.

At that time I was also running a little business from our apartment. Everything in New York had a T-shirt printed with its name – the bars, the restaurants, the schools and even the churches – and, not one to miss an opportunity I was printing T-shirts in our bedroom with the screen-printing machine taking up most of the space!

I advertised in the *Irish Echo* and printed T-shirts in the colours of each Irish county with the county name written in Gaelic. I had not a word of Irish, as only the A class in the secondary school learnt it and it took me three years to get to that class so it was too late to start. Ruth was at university in Coleraine and was called upon for the spellings. She was always a great girl to get information and she supplied me with the county colours as well. We did not make a fortune but the machines were nearly paid for by the time we were going home.

A man once called me from the west coast and asked, 'Are these shirts Irish made?'

'Well,' said I, always quick with an answer, 'I'm Irish and I make them.'

He laughed, 'Okay, that will do me.'

I had approached Barry McGuigan the previous time I was home to see if he wanted to have his face printed on a T-shirt, which was what the American sports stars where doing. Barry was training for the world title boxing championship at the time and as my brother had roofed his house I had a way in. One of the great advantages of coming from a big family is that everyone knows a lot of people.

Off I went as bold as brass to Barry and told him what I was thinking. He said to make samples and send them to him. I got photos and his signature and we decided what I would work from. I printed one with his face on it, one with his signature across it and the third with a cyclone coming down the middle with 'Barry McGuigan, the Clones Cyclone' on it. Proud of my designs, I sent them to him but didn't hear a word back.

Marty continued to work in construction as I prepared to move. I knew we would have to make a living at home and decided to bring my business with me. With the big day for departure on the horizon I packed all I wanted and had my machines picked up to be shipped home as they were a fraction of the price I would have to pay for them there.

All thoughts of Barry McGuigan had gone and I was getting ready to go over to see friends to say goodbye when the phone rang.

'Is this Mary?' a lady asked

When I replied that I was, she said, 'This is Sandra McGuigan, Barry's wife. Are you still printing T-shirts?'

When I told her I was she said, 'Well, you know Barry is fighting in the World Championship soon and I was wondering if you would print the T-shirts for it?'

'No problem!' I said without hesitation, even though I had not a notion how I was going to manage without machines.

'I thought you didn't get the ones I sent or that you did not like them,' I said, curious as to why she was calling now.

'I've been wearing them all the time,' she said, 'and everyone is asking me where I got them and if I could I get more.'

We chatted for a while and I told her I would call her in the next few days as I was going back to Ireland the following day. Panic should have set in but, when it comes to business, I never was a worrier. Off I went out and thought, 'I'll sort this out when I get home.'

A few days later I met Sandra and she said she wanted thousands of T-shirts. I had no contact with anyone in this business at home so I asked her for one of the shirts that they were selling at that time. It said, 'Here we go, Here we go, Here we go,' which was the chant to be heard at all Barry's fights.

The only information I could glean from that T-shirt was the fact that it was made in Brazil. Not wanting to look unprofessional I told Sandra I would get back to her with a price, as I had no idea what the costs were on this side of the Atlantic.

Off I went back to Mammy's, where I was staying, as Marty wasn't due home for a week. That's when the panic set in; not mine, but Mammy's.

'Where are you going to get all those T-shirts to print and how are you going to get them printed before the fight next week in London?' she fretted.

Funny how only one person needs to fret at any given time.

'Give me the phone and I'll sort it out,' I said. We had now had this long-awaited luxury to keep us in contact with the rest of the world.

Making use of the one clue on the T-shirt I called the Brazilian Embassy in London and asked them how I would find out who imported these T-shirts from their country. Within minutes I had the number of a company in Brighton. It's amazing how you can think when you stay calm.

I called the number as Mam ran around cleaning the house to

settle herself. A lady answered and I explained what I wanted.

'One moment please,' she said as she connected me with an extension.

'What can I do for you?' said a man with a Dublin accent,

Again I explained what I wanted and he said, 'Here we go, Here we go, Here we go.'

He explained that they were the company that printed Barry's last shirts.

'Have you got the designs?' he asked.

'Yes,' I replied.

'Well, send them over to me,' he said.

I had not a notion of sending my designs to anyone, even if he was from Dublin. 'I'll come over with them,' I said.

Down went the phone and as I started to dial again, out came Mam, who had been cleaning around the door of the hall, listening.

'What are you doing now?' she asked with a worried face.

'Booking a ticket to go to London. I can stay with Frances and take the train down to Brighton.'

Next morning I was on the road to Belfast in the new VW van that Dad had ordered before I came home. Maroon was its colour, which Dad had picked without consulting me. It was the first time I bought a vehicle and I didn't know I had a choice. When I asked him why he chose maroon he said the salesman said it was the most popular colour, which would have completely turned me off as I am never interested in the most popular anything.

I called Frances, a friend from school, and booked my bed for the night. Frances was pregnant at the time and we sat and chatted half the night about the secondary school where we met, wondering where all our friends were now.

I headed to Brighton on a train early next morning to buy five thousand T-shirts. During the conversation the previous day the Dub had asked if I wanted them printed. I said I would print them myself even though my machines had not even left New York. My curious nature led me to ask how much the company charged for printing and I nearly dropped the phone when he gave me a price. It was so low that I could not do it at the same price if I had the whole family working around the clock for nothing. That's when the light came on and things started to look up and I knew all I had to do was trust.

At the factory I met the big smiling Dub and he agreed not only to have them done on time for the fight the following week but to have them delivered to the stadium on the day. So the business was concluded and off I went back to the airport and home to a happy and relieved Mammy.

Marty arrived home a few days later, to a house I had rented on the Sligo coast. When I say the coast, I mean the *coast,* as you could be in the water in two minutes flat if you were strong enough to face it. It was freezing. We could look out from the bed and see the Atlantic. I loved it but Marty wasn't so keen. The silence was deafening and he missed the noise of New York City.

The following week the pair of us went off to London to the fight. I had really no interest in boxing but I did want to see all the people wearing the T-shirts I had designed.

When talking to Sandra the first day I asked her if she thought Barry would win.

'Of course!' she answered.

'Why don't we print an extra thousand with 'Barry McGuigan, World Champion' on them?' I suggested.

She agreed and that's exactly what we did.

Barry won the fight and what a night it was and what a time for Clones when he got back.

It was coming into the winter and the transfer of the farm was not yet finalised so I called Lorna in New York and asked if she wanted a companion for her mother over the winter months in Florida. She said that would be great so we packed again, left our new van in storage and headed back across the Atlantic. In America I spent my time taking care of Mae while Marty worked again in construction.

7

Maybe You Don't Need
to Win the Lottery

I had just returned from working in Florida. Marty had come back weeks before and found us a house in a little village in Roscommon which was close enough to the farm that we were in the process of buying from his mother.

The house was a so-called 'modern bungalow' but you could not heat if you left all the radiators on 24/7 and after returning from a hot climate I had no choice but to sit on top of a fire. I would have had more benefit had I sat on the chimney pot, wearing every stitch of clothes I could put on me.

Marty had picked me up from Shannon on the Thursday morning and two days later after the jet lag had eased a little I went up to the local phone box to call home. After six years out of the country I was ready to settle into the peace of living in the west, where my husband had been born. I had dreamt of this and had finally convinced Marty to come back so we could rear our children, who had yet to be born. I dreamed we would do this in the peace and beauty of the west.

The little village consisted of two pubs, two shops and a church and was really beautiful. The ruin of the castle of the O'Connor clan overlooked it. The ideal place, I thought, to start a new life. We had been married nearly three years at this time and had saved all our money for this idyllic life.

As I stepped into the phone box I was looking forward to talking to Mam and telling her I would be up home later that day.

My brother Noel answered the phone. I was full of the joys of spring that morning and ready for a chat.

He just asked, 'Are you coming home?' And when I said yes. he said, 'Well, come home now,' and put the phone down.

Annoyed and puzzled I called back and asked, 'Can I speak to Mammy?'

'No,' he said, 'she's in bed. Just come home.'

I rushed back to Marty and threw a few clothes into a bag, telling him that I had to get home because something was wrong with Mammy.

The six years out of the country had left me with no real interest in the national news. I had been brought up listening to news on the hour and was sick of it. Living in America and listening to the news there did not encourage me to listen. When I read their version of the Troubles, I knew they had no idea of what they were talking about and figured if they got this one so wrong they probably had most everything else wrong too.

I put a cassette in the recorder as I negotiated the twisty back-roads of Roscommon into Cavan. I was only half-listening to what was on as I thought of my mother, a strong brave woman who saw a doctor only when she really needed to – which was not often.

The cassette finished, I flipped it out to turn it over and the newsreader said, 'Two men have been shot on the Monaghan-Fermanagh border. One is dead, one very seriously wounded.'

I knew one of them was one of my seven brothers. I don't know how I knew, but I knew.

'Noel answered the phone,' I thought as I eliminated them. 'Paddy is in London, Tom and Peter in New York. Kevin is in Long Kesh. It's not Brendie and Seán would not cross the border. Would he?'

It was then I knew. Seán had been shot.

As I turned into the lane at home one of the neighbours pulled up his car, rolled down his window and asked, 'How is Seán?'

'Was it Seán?' I replied.

'I don't know,' he answered and drove off like a bat out of hell.

I got to the house where Gertie, the youngest of the family, was in bits. The police had been calling all morning saying, 'We got him and he is going to die,' and laughing. She was seventeen. The rest of the family was at the hospital.

I could not see Seán. Police surrounded the hospital and he was being rushed to a hospital in Belfast. I waited for Seamus's body to be removed, then made my way back to my shattered dreams of peace in the west of Ireland.

My mother-in-law was a shrewd lady and I knew she would put two and two together.

I asked my mother what I should say to the in-laws.

'Tell them you didn't know him.'

I knew she wanted to protect me but I was not prepared to deny my brother to make someone else feel better. Having an active Republican in the family was far from cool, especially if your in-laws had married into the security forces in the South.

The following day as I drove with Marty to the farm, he agreed with Mammy that I should tell his mother nothing. I decided I wouldn't say anything but that I would not deny it if asked. I knew quite well she would ask.

We sat on the two sides of the fire as Marty checked his animals. The headlines of all the Sunday papers read 'Two Republicans shot in shoot-to-kill policy by the SAS.'

'Terrible shooting in Fermanagh,' she said.

'Yes,' I replied

'Up your country.'

'Yes.'

'One of them was Lynch.'

'Yes.'

'Did you know him?'

'He's my brother.'

'Oh your poor mother,' she said.

'Just thank the Lord every day that you did not have to raise your children in Northern Ireland,' I replied.

It was never mentioned again.

Seán and Seamus McElwain were shot on the Fermanagh-Monaghan border while they were on active service as members of the IRA. The SAS, an elite military undercover unit, was lying in wait. They opened fire without warning as they crossed a ditch. Seamus fell to the ground whilst Seán, seriously wounded, ran on knowing if it was the SAS they would take no prisoners. He had already been shot in the stomach and side and as he ran he was hit in the leg. He crossed into another field and ran on until, unable to continue, he found a place to conceal himself to avoid detection. Fifteen minutes later Seán heard three more shots ring out, Seamus was shot as he lay on the ground after being questioned.

Seán lay motionless face-down in the drain for two hours, while they searched for him in vain. Finally the SAS left. Very few people would wish to be captured but Seán said he did, knowing that as time passed he would die of his injuries.

He was found by a British soldier with a dog who said, 'Have you been shot, mate?'

'I've been riddled,' he answered.

The soldier went to get help. In the meantime the RUC arrived and kicked Seán viciously as he squealed with pain. One put a foot on his chest and a rifle to his head while another policeman said, 'Don't shoot him, just let him die.'

Seán said, 'I am a solider of war and shouldn't be treated with brutality.'

When the army doctor arrived he told them to stop mistreating him as it was no way to treat a seriously injured person. He ordered six of them to take him carefully out of the ditch. Then he tended to his wounds and told the RUC to watch carefully as the experience might come in useful some day if any of their colleagues was ever injured.

Sean was taken to the Erne Hospital in Enniskillen for a six-hour operation, from there to the intensive care unit in the Royal Hospital, Belfast, and from there to Musgrave Park Hospital, where he spent the next two months recovering.

Seamus was one of the most wanted men in Ireland at the time; he was one of the thirty-eight political prisoners who had escaped from Long Kesh in 1983. Seán was on the run in the South, living in Clones with his wife and young son.

After his recovery, he was sentenced to twenty-five years in Long Kesh and became one of the OCs (commanding officer of the political prisoners) that followed a line that included Bobby Sands. He was released two and a half weeks before his time was up, under the Good Friday Agreement, and was spokesperson for the Republican prisoners in Long Kesh at the time of the Peace Agreement.

Since his release Seán has worked tirelessly to advance the Sinn Féin peace strategy. He had often said to me that he would not want his son or future generations to have to go through what we went through.

He was also one of the first Republican ex-prisoners to become a member of the DPP (District Policing Board), a civic forum to hold the newly-formed PSNI to account. This has earned him national media attention.

While writing this book I went walking with a group in the mountains, including Seán. We talked about everything, including the latest recession, as we walked through the long, thick heather of Slieve Anierin. As we approached one of the peaks, I asked him, 'Do you ever do the lottery?'

'No,' he answered 'I don't need to. I have already won it, I survived.'

8

DON'T FORCE ANYTHING:
IT WILL WORK ITSELF OUT IN ITS OWN TIME

As Seán lay recovering in the hospital, I tried to get on as normally as possible back in Roscommon, getting any information I could via the local phone box, which I was beginning to feel belonged to me alone. Seán improved slowly but he improved.

I tried to get my business off the ground when the machines finally arrived from New York, via China I think. They took a long time and were then held up by customs in Dublin. In the meantime I tried to drum up a little business but all kinds of problems had reared their heads.

I decided to do a start-your-own-business course in Galway, which was funded at the time, and an excellent course. We were interviewed for this and I got my place. The first morning the interviewer came straight over to my desk and asked me to come to his office. 'My God,' I thought, 'what have I done now!'

In I went and he told me to close the door. 'Mary,' he said, 'we have an inspector coming in this morning and if he asks what age you are, tell him you are twenty-five.' (I was twenty-six.)

'Not again!' I thought. 'How many more lies do I have to tell?'

I was just back from New York where I had been illegal for more than six years, travelling over and back with the aid of two passports and two visas. One of the benefits of being from the North was that we were of dual nationality and could hold two passports. We could then get two visas, which meant we used a different passport every time we entered the States. It was simply as if we were two different people.

I lied every time I crossed the border when I was asked where I was going by the army or police, and now here I was back at home, living in the Free State, legal and with my own name and I was being asked to lie about my age! 'Why?' I asked.

'You are a year too old for this course because it is funded for the under twenty-fives but I want you on it as I know of the twenty people out there you are the one who will actually start her own business.'

'Thank you,' was all I could say. I wasn't asked my age.

Seán got better, Kevin got out and the next few years passed with a lot more raids and arrests and loads of tension up at home.

Life went on and so did the war. I could never understand why it was called the 'Troubles', when men and woman were arrested, held until their trial without bail, tried in front of a judge with no jury and by this time demanding to be called political prisoners. This suited all those in power but I wondered if so many men and women were killed in Connacht would it be considered the 'Troubles'.

We had moved from that big, cold, modern bungalow to a small three-bedroomed cottage in the country when I realised I was pregnant. We were both delighted. I spent my days up and down to the farm helping Marty and my nights watching Stephen Roche win the Tour de France. Pregnancy suited me. I'd prance around with my tummy out so everyone would notice. I was small and thin and looked like what a neighbour said I would if ever I was pregnant. My bump looked like a knot on a rope.

I decided I wanted to have my baby in Enniskillen and I diligently made the long journey to keep doctors' appointments. The roads were bad, with twists and turns that would make you dizzy, and the journey took a lot longer than it should have done.

Crossing the border at that time was an episode in itself. You were stopped, questioned and sometimes searched and held. Luck was on my side and they never seemed to figure out who I was. Fermanagh, unlike most of the Six Counties, had very few Republican families so we would have been well known to the security forces.

Driving up in my Galway registered car (I taxed it there, rather than have a Roscommon number plate, as this resulted in the army continually asking what county it was in), I did as little as possible to draw any attention to myself.

One cold frosty morning I waited my turn at the checkpoint, in a rush as usual for my appointment.

'What's your name?' the young solider asked.

'Mary Geraghty,' I sweetly replied.

He looked at me, went into his hut, came back out and said, 'I know who you are.'

My heart stopped. Christ, I thought, I am going to be held here, as most of my family had become accustomed to happening to them. 'You're the girl from Lisnaskea that married the farmer from Galway.'

'Yes. That's exactly who I am.' I drove on, shaking. Being married to Marty was a great camouflage. In all the time my journeys took me across the border or indeed throughout the Free State it was my security, my right of way.

The pregnancy went wonderfully well. The week my baby was due we were to do a trial run to Enniskillen, just in case, but of course Marty was tied up at the farm and we could not go.

We lived across the road from a strange little lady whom I visited regularly. She lived in a two-storey house by herself, sat over the open hearth every day, smoked cigarettes and told me stories. She was one of those elderly people in the west who fascinated me, one of those hardy people who rode a bicycle to town a few days a week to do their shopping, something that was not such a regular sight in the North. She did not use much water in her personal hygiene but we'd sit there and chat about all kinds of things.

That particular evening, with no sign of Marty, I wandered over to Mae and was leaning over the open fire when the 6 o'clock news came on. 'Massive Bomb in Enniskillen,' was the headline. I watched as people were pulled from the wreckage and thought that we were supposed to be there.

Gordon Wilson said about the death of his daughter, 'I bear no ill-will. I bear no grudge.' I remember thinking I could never do that. I couldn't forgive the people who terrorised us. The wall that I had built around me meant that I did not feel as much as I should have but I thought at the time that this was good.

The following Thursday, with not a budge from the baby, I went to the hospital to be induced on the Friday, which was the local custom. The town was like a scene from a war movie but strangely, like the southerners who did not recognise the war, I was blind to the reality of it.

The doctor who saw me said he didn't believe I would deliver a baby next day even after being induced – but he was wrong. I was in the labour ward first thing next morning wriggling in pain. It was Friday 13 November. 'Are you superstitious?' the nurse asked, as she wheeled me down the corridor.

'I don't know,' I said, 'but I consider Friday the thirteenth a lucky day.'

It was; my beautiful daughter was born. I had convinced myself I was going to have a boy as somewhere deep in my subconscious I thought boys came first. Maybe I thought they would mind the girls. I've no idea where that crazy notion had come from because the women of our family are very independent, which came from being raised by a very strong mother.

Anyway Roisín was born: long, thin, beautiful and cold – so she was rushed to the incubator. Marty went with her as I was being stitched. 'Christ,' I thought, 'I'm glad the nurse was so wrong. At a quarter to four when I screamed with pain, she said, 'Don't fret, it will be all over in a few hours. Should be born by six.'

I cried, thinking I would never stick it for another two hours, but Roisín was born ten minutes later.

At that time the maternity ward in the Erne Hospital was like a prison and you were not discharged for a week. In one way I was very glad. At my age I had enough wit to know the responsibility I had just taken on. I needed more than the nine months to get used to it. I needed the help of the nurses and they were great. I was also glad to be in the local hospital because my family and neighbours came in to see me all the time and gave me the usual advice.

But that week the Erne Hospital in Enniskillen was not the most pleasant place to be. The country was in shock, the town was in shock. I think everybody who worked in the hospital was traumatised and it was indescribable. The morgue was holding eleven bodies and the wards were full of people who were injured both physically and emotionally.

The break came for a lot of people when Prince Charles and Lady Di came to visit. There were only a few new babies so we were asked to come out and meet them both. Leaving my baby at the side of the bed, I went alone and hoped there would be no press around, as pictures of me shaking hands with Royalty was not something my mother would not approve of under any circumstances. I had a bed booked in her new house to be minded for the next week, a privilege I would not have forsaken for anyone – not even a prince and princess – but thankfully there was no one there but Charles and Di.

I remember thinking, 'What an unhappy couple!' He was pleasant but she was one of the most miserable people I had ever encountered. Years later I remember a reporter saying he had met her on that very day and what a beautiful, charming woman she was and I thought maybe she could be miserable around us when there was no need for a show. Later I would do this myself – put on a show for people.

Home I went to Mam and Dad, all seven-and-a-half stone of me, like a wraith. They minded me for the week. It was heaven, as it always is staying with them, but especially after that week in the hospital where I think even the babies were traumatised.

I was my Mammy's baby and Roisín was mine and we had a lovely time. The following Sunday, she was rushed to the church to be baptised, as Dad said that you should never visit a child until it was baptised. I think deep down he feared that I might not bother, so she was duly baptised in the local church with Dad and Mam her godparents. The priest there left the church a few weeks later and Dad always maintained that she was not really baptised at all.

I returned to the west with my baby to start a new life and a new business and tried my best to forget all the things I did not yet have the strength to remember.

9

SET YOUR EYE ON YOUR GOAL, NOT ON THE RECESSION

I went to the States with my mother for a visit in 1979 and returned there in 1980 to work. Aunt Lucy, whom we went to visit in 1979 told me it was pointless to think of coming back to the States as they had a 'recession'. I was only twenty at the time and didn't know the meaning of the word so I ignored her.

My daughter, who is finishing her degree in Media and has just turned twenty-one, recently asked me. 'How would you define a recession, Mam?'

I replied, 'Roisín, a recession is when the waitress has a degree and counts herself lucky to have a job.' That's how it was in New York in the 1980s.

In 1980 when I landed in New York there were very few Irish there and very few jobs. I saw an advertisement in the local Irish paper for nurse's aids and got myself on the books of an Irish nursing agency. I was never trained in any of this work but I had always wanted to be a nurse and was in charge of the doctor's box at home when we were growing up and I figured that would do. The doctor's box was a biscuit tin where Mammy kept the bandages and I was the doctor in our house.

I remember my first job as a nurse's aid; it was in the Doctor's Hospital in mid-town Manhattan. My job was to sit at the side of the bed of an elderly man and get him whatever he needed – a nurse, a drink – or help him to sit out.

Of course I also had to take his temperature, which I had not a clue how to do. A thermometer did not exist in our doctor's box and I never saw one until I left home. When I was first asked to do it I picked up the phone from the side of the man's bed and rang Ann, the nurse I was now living with in the Bronx, and that was sorted. Taking his blood pressure was a bigger problem!

I went to houses and apartments all over New York City to take care of the elderly at any time of day or night and never refused a job. I enjoyed it and I got to know the city. I had no idea how long I would do it but it paid the bills.

Then I met Lorna and Mae and ended up with a great job in real estate in Manhattan.

In 1981 the young Irish started to come to New York as the recession had hit Ireland and things were starting to look up in the States. By 1983 they were thick on the streets of the Bronx where I lived. When we got married ninety-five Irish people attended our wedding in New York and ninety of them were illegal. The priest was an American cousin of mine and he made a joke about President Reagan giving us all an amnesty.

There was plenty of work and the Irish were popular in New York. We were white and good workers and spoke English. If you were not a good worker, you went home. 'Period,' as the Americans would say.

There was no such thing as social security or benefits of any kind. We were illegal aliens and the only benefit you would get would be from a friend who would keep you for a few weeks but only a few weeks. If you could not get work or did not want to work, you went home.

The day after Roisín was christened in the North, we went back to the west and finished negotiations on a house in a local town. When Roisín was six months old we moved again.

Marty and I had lived in New York, Florida, Sligo, Belfast, Dublin and two different houses in Roscommon and I was truly sick of moving. I remember his brother-in-law Paddy smiling as he asked, 'How long to intend to stay here?

'A stick of gelignite won't move me again until I have my children reared,' I replied.

The house was a split-level bungalow at the edge of a small town, Marty said we couldn't afford it and he was right. We had the three thousand pounds for the deposit but I borrowed the first month's mortgage from Dad and Mam until I got something off the ground.

It had three flats in the basement and I knew it was exactly what I wanted. I would somehow make enough money so I would not have to go out to work. I could raise my children myself and still have my own income. I had no idea how I was going to do this in a recession but that was never a problem before and it never entered my mind that it would be a problem now.

I knew one person in that town: he was from Fermanagh and Dad had spotted him in the chapel one Sunday when he was down. Paddy had played football with Dad and was the sweetest man you ever could meet. Unfortunately he died a few months later.

I painted the house by day, Paddy's wife Freda minded Roisín and Paddy duly brought her up to me when she was hungry, as I was breastfeeding. He would bring her back to Freda when she had finished. I painted and painted downstairs because that was the area I intended to make a living from. Gertie came to help me paint. She was eighteen at the time. She asked me one day as we painted the small bathroom, 'What are you going to do with this place?'

'I don't know yet.'

'What if you can't get something started?'

'Did Mrs Browne [our Domestic Science teacher] not teach you that there is no such thing as "can't"?'

That's another thing that still rings in my mind about Mrs Browne – plus the fact that she told me to use elbow grease and I wondered where I would get it.

With the experience of working as a nurse's aid in New York I thought I would take in a few old people and mind them to make enough to pay the mortgage and buy the groceries.

At the time the local psychiatric hospital was closing down and they were boarding out the patients. Paddy suggested I go to enquire if I could board a few of them out. It was not quite what I had in mind but my desire to be at home with my children was stronger than any wish. Paddy and I went to visit a man from the hospital, Jimmy, who told me they had all been boarded out.

I left disheartened but continued to paint and use the money I had received after selling my T-shirt printing machines. I sold them because I had problems importing T-shirts. Most of the money went to instal central heating into the flats to get ready for the rush of old people at my door looking for accommodation.

Paddy died shortly after that and after drinking brandy at his wake I staggered through my own door. I had only one drink – I could never drink – but Freda insisted. Marty said Jimmy from the hospital was on the phone. 'Jimmy who'? I asked?

'From the psychiatric hospital,' he replied, as I took the phone.

'Would you take two psychiatric patients?' Jimmy asked.

'Can I see them?'

'Yes and we want to see where you intend to put them.'

The next day I went to the hospital and met Jimmy and Martin and thought, 'I'll have no problem minding you two.'

My house was checked and looked good after a few months of hard work. The men moved in next day, along with a man I had already booked in through an advertisement in the local paper. Over the next few weeks the health board filled my house and I was earning a lot more than I had expected as the recession continued.

Jimmy told me that one of the men had been in the hospital for thirty-five years. 'If he stays with you for a week he'll stay a long time.' This man moved out of my house eighteen years later when he was over eighty and needed to go into a home for more care.

Over the next twenty years I stayed at home, ran a business and was there for my children. I never thought it would be any different. I never did see the recession, just the goal.

10

See the Funny Side

My second pregnancy went just as well as my first. Again I thrived but this time my bump was far from being like a knot on a rope. I put weight on everywhere and must have been nearly eleven stone when I was due, which was a lot on my tiny frame. We were both delighted as getting pregnant was not as easy for me as I had expected.

Working from home was great but it was never-ending. Marty was gone most of the time and with Roisín a toddler and into everything, I was exhausted. I remember the day she came into the bedroom where I had lain down for forty winks and said, 'I eat the tablets.'

Well I was pretty sure she didn't but could take no chances. Greg, our doctor, told me I'd have to bring her to the hospital to be checked out. It must have been one of the wettest weeks this country has ever seen as I negotiated the floods. I drove the more than forty miles alone as Marty was tied up with lambing season.

I sat at her bedside and tried to sleep in a hard chair. It was a long night but I did get a camp bed close to the morning and was very grateful for it. Leaving the hospital grounds the next morning, I tipped a car as I reversed out in a daze but never heard from the owner. I think he must have seen how stressed-out I was.

Two months later I was back in the same hospital. I had come to adjust to life in the west and having my baby there. Greg sent me in when he reckoned I was in labour but they didn't agree with him and after a night there they sent me the long journey home again. I paced the floors at home all day, then went back to Greg. He examined me and sent me back, telling me I would have a baby before ten in the morning.

My sister Lucy, a trained masseuse, was staying with me so I asked her to massage every place she could to induce me, as this time I had no intention of coming back home without a baby.

We were back on the road and arrived at the maternity unit after midnight that night.

Everything was closed down and we had to ring a bell. 'What do you want?' a voice asked from the intercom.

'For God's sake'! said Lucy. 'What the hell do they think we want ringing the door of the maternity ward at nearly one o'clock in the morning!' A long time in New York had made her as blunt as any New Yorker.

I thought it might be just as well to deal with this situation on my own and sent her home. I got a bed and thankfully lay down but not long after the pains became unbearable. I rang the bell and the nurse sent for a doctor.

'Do you think she might have a kidney infection?' she asked him.

'God!' I thought, 'do they not understand? I'm nine months pregnant and in labour!' Maybe sending Lucy home was not one of my brightest ideas.

Well, it was a long night. I hung on to the bars of the headboard and tried to make as little noise as possible until I couldn't bear it any more and rang the bell again.

'Is this your first child?' the nurse asked for the second time.

'No, and the first one shot out very fast.'

The morning eventually arrived and in came another doctor who asked, 'Would you mind if I did another internal?'

This was probably the sixth in the past two days but at this point I did not care what they did with me.

'I don't think she's in labour,' said the nurse, smiling sweetly at the doctor.

'Maybe not,' he replied, 'but the baby is on its way out.'

I was rushed to the labour ward where a lovely wee nurse was left with me.

Ten minutes later in came herself again. 'Nurse, we need you next door,' she said.

'No,' I screamed, 'I don't want to be left alone.' And I hung on to the kind nurse's arm.

Thank God, this time I won. The bossy one left and ten minutes later my baby was born, at ten minutes to ten.

'What do you have at home?' the nurse asked.

'A girl.'

'Well, now you have one of each.'

'I don't believe it. I thought I was carrying a girl!'

'It sure looks like a boy to me!'

When she gave him to me to feed, I was very happy as he looked up at me with his big round face, the picture of my mother.

Great, I thought, I don't have to come back here again if I don't want to. Marty has his farmer.

Marty arrived a few hours later. I was alone in a ward that had to be opened for the overflow of patients but I was very happy and Marty was delighted.

'What will we call him?' he asked

'I thought you wanted to call him Jarlath.'

'Well, what do you want?'

'Roisín was my choice so I'll leave it to you.'

Roisín was my only choice for a girl's name. I had loved the name all my life. To be very honest I would have agreed to anything. I was so happy it was over and all was well.

Out came the pen. Marty wrote Jarlath on a piece of paper and asked me for a name.

Oisin would have been my first choice for a boy but I thought Roisín and Oisin might be a bit much in one family as Roisín was pronounced in the northern fashion, which was Oisin with a 'R'.

Fergal, I wrote, and Ruairí, as Marty had now produced another name.

The names were rolled up individually and put in a beaker that had been left on the locker beside my bed.

Marty pulled out Fergal. 'I don't know if I like that name,' he said with a worried face.

'Can we just call him Jarlath and get on with it please?' I said. 'It's what you want.'

Jarlath was the name of one of Marty's best friends, who was killed two years later crossing a street in New York. One of the greatest characters you could ever meet and a man we all loved.

Ruth, my younger sister, arrived a little later to see her new nephew before heading to Australia the next day. She is five years younger than me and had neither chick nor child at the time. She looked me up and down as I waddled out to the door with her after the visit. 'Are you sure you don't have another one in there?'

I could have killed her. I knew I still looked nine months

pregnant but did not want to be reminded and I thought, 'I'll get you back some day.' I had to wait ten years before I could return the compliment to her.

Later that evening, in came my least favourite nurse. 'Can't believe you had the baby so fast this morning,' she said.

Well, I thought, maybe if you had been listening to me in the middle of night you would have heard me say I was a fast producer.

'Are you staying with us for the next few days?' she asked.

'No, I'm going home tomorrow.'

'I don't think you'll be ready,' she continued.

Well, I thought, I might have had a problem getting in here but I will not have a problem getting out. I know where the door is.

Two years later I was rushed into hospital with an unbearable pain and on my thirty-third birthday was operated on for an ectopic pregnancy. The tube was removed with the foetus.

The following day the doctor who did the operation came to see me. She told me I had the worst tubes she had ever seen and that I was a very lucky woman to have any children. Two months later my other tube was removed.

11

Loss and Gain

When I had my operation for the ectopic pregnancy I felt the whole thing was treated very casually. I did not know I was pregnant one day and the next I had the foetus removed with my tube. Amen, over, finished and not another word about it.

The nuns ran the hospital where the operation took place and ran it extremely well but I was never asked how I felt, how I really felt. As far as everyone was concerned I had had an operation and was lucky to have the pregnancy detected, I was lucky to be alive. But I knew I had lost a baby, the second baby I had lost.

The first was a miscarriage in the States years before. Marty and I had been staying with my aunt and I was very sick one day with terrible pains. I thought it was a very heavy period and it was years later when my sister-in-law was describing the miscarriage she had had that I realised what had happened to me that day.

Not only had I lost a baby this time but a fallopian tube. I was advised to go back and have the second one removed so I lost the ability to have any more children.

I counted my blessings. I had two beautiful healthy children and was back working a few days later but I felt a huge loss that again was buried in work. When I did get around to healing my past it included this loss. I grieved for my two children, who were never meant to be born but were part of me. I felt in no man's land until I sorted this out.

Not knowing how one deals with this and not knowing if anyone did, I did it through my meditations. I set the time aside and I went back to each time and visualised it happening again but this time I stayed with my babies and held them and told them how much I loved them. In fact I kept them with me for days and every time I meditated I would go into the little room that I created for them, where I could bond with them before I said goodbye.

I never had any doubt in my mind the sex of each of them. The first was a little girl and I called her Sarah, the second a little boy whom I named Jack. I knew when the wound in me had healed and I took them both at different times and buried them under a tree in my mind, a tree in the park where I knew I could go and visit them every day on my walk.

It was not a problem for me to visualise all this without anyone else knowing what was going on in my head, as visualising had by this time become part of my life. I was in mourning and I grieved for my loss and could then let them go to their rest. It was my healing process and it worked for me. I told no one, as I doubted if they would understand.

Years later when my marriage had broken up and things were really getting on top of me I decided to take a holiday alone. Dad and Mam came down and took over my house and kids and I went to Lanzarote for a week. I knew I needed to be alone for the week, away from everything and everyone.

When I first had the idea that I wanted to get away I called my elder sister, whom I could always rely on to be honest and direct.

'Geraldine,' I said, 'I was thinking of going on holidays on my own.'

'Well, what's the problem?' she asked.

'Should I go on my own?'

'That depends. Are you going on your own because you want to be on your own or are you going on your own because you have no one to go with you?'

'I'm going on my own because I want to be on my own,' I immediately replied.

'So what's the problem?'

There wasn't one after that. I knew I needed time alone but it had been so long since I had been alone that I was a little nervous. But I had a feeling I was going to meet someone.

I said this to my friend Caroline. 'Oh!' she said, her eyes twinkling, 'do you think you will meet a man?'

'No,' I answered without thinking, 'it's a woman.'

Dad and Mam arrived the day before I was to go so they could settle in and get all sorted. I had called Mammy and said I needed a break away on my own and without hesitation she said, 'Book a holiday and we'll take over.' To be honest I was surprised but she knew that I was going through a lot as any mother knows, even if she did not ask any questions.

Dad and Mam had been coming to me for years, more than they went to any of their other children. Every time I was sick – which was a lot before I finally took the time to sort myself out – or when we wanted to go on holiday they would be there for me.

On the way to my house, Mammy would always stop in Jack's shop at the bottom of the road and buy Parazone, Brillo pads and cloths. I often felt Jack must think I have the dirtiest house in the country but that's what Mammy loved to do: clean. It was her way of keeping sane and my house was her place to run when she could take no more of the Troubles as I was the only one living south of the border. I never complained because I was always left with a spring-cleaned house when she left.

By this time there was no one living at home with them but always someone coming and going. I think Mam's body hadn't got used to doing nothing after twelve children and my house was the closest thing to the home she knew best, a very busy one. There were eight patients, two adults and two children living there and we made up her twelve. The only difference for her was that she came like a whirlwind and left when she wanted and it really suited us both very well.

When she was cleaning I could catch up with all the things I did not usually have the time for: cutting hair, doing feet and nails, buying clothes and all the extras that came with my big fostered family.

The west was free and it was where my parents found their few days to escape when they needed to. Dad would come in berating governments, police, soldiers and politicians. I would listen and say nothing and an hour later when he had said it all he would go to my garden, like a child playing with the toy it loved best. I say 'my' garden but it was his as I knew nothing about it. I had too much to do and I left it to him. Sometimes I would be surprised at the things that appeared there, like the time I came back after a few days away and found tulips growing in a circle around a rock; tulips he had planted the year before and had not even mentioned. They were beautiful.

This time they were back and they loved the idea that they were in charge for a week, Dad would say that you could be in the kitchen cooking all the time that you were not cleaning and he was right. When I was not cooking and cleaning I would be painting or renovating properties that I had bought to keep me busy.

Off I went to Knock airport, excited to be alone for a week but also scared of being lonely – lonely for my children. A friend, Mary, left me to the airport and introduced me to people she knew who were going to the same resort. I got their number just in case anything happened to me and I needed someone.

I had chosen Lanzarote for two reasons: I had been there a few times before and felt I knew the place and would feel safe there; and I would not have to go to the airport in Dublin. Knock was just down the road and I could be dropped off in twenty minutes.

When I reached my seat I noticed I was in the middle, which meant the people on either side of me were not together. I said hello to both of them: a woman in the window seat and a young boy in the aisle seat. When I had settled myself the woman to my left said, 'My name is Anne and this is my first time to go on holidays on my own.'

I laughed and said, 'I'm Mary and this is my first time too. I have done a lot of travelling alone but this is my first time to go on a package holiday alone.' We chatted on the way over and agreed to meet for dinner the next night.

I checked in at my apartment building and made my way to the unit where I was to spend the next week. I threw my bags in the bedroom and headed out for food and to make a call home to my parents and kids.

Later that night I settled my self into the single bed in the twin-bedded room and drifted off to sleep. I woke in the middle of the night with the feeling that someone was in the room with me, someone not human but with a lovely energy so I was not afraid.

I sat up in the dark and knew right away that it was my children who had come to visit, the two children I had lost and I immediately understood that I was to spend my week with them, which I did.

It was as if I was not alone: they came everywhere with me. As I lay on the beach they were there with me. When I went out to dinner they were there and I talked to them all the time. It was wonderful therapy for me and by the time I got home they were part of my life even though they were on a different plane.

The second night I met Anne for dinner. I told her what was happening and she understood, as I knew she would. She had trained as a therapist and had been taught to do what I had done intuitively. Anne and I became firm friends that night. We are friends to this day and hardly a day passes that I don't speak to her on the phone.

I think this was the first time I truly realised that we could connect to a higher power for help, even if we were not religious. I had a wonderfully restful, healing week and went home with strength to face anything and with the knowledge that I had two little helpers.

Later I told my children on this earth about our little guardian angels and if I ever feel either of them need help I ask the help of their brother and sister. 'Sarah,' I say, 'keep an eye on Roisín,' or, 'Jack, keep an eye on Jarlath.' I may have lost two children not meant for this life but I gained two that were meant for another.

12

Chopping Wood and Drawing Water

There is an old Chinese saying: 'I'm chopping wood and drawing water.' It's what you do when you have to keep going to survive. When I did get time in my busy life to visit the North, I tried to get to see both Seán and Kevin as much as possible. They were now serving time together in Long Kesh.

I hated that long road up the M1 and that miserable waiting room, a prefab where you were searched and then left waiting with God knows who. Nobody knew who anyone was until the names of the prisoners were called: then you had a good idea of what side they came from.

The visitors would get on the bus together in silence, a bus like a tin box with tin windows and no view out. The only thing you were aware of was the ramps you crossed to get to the other waiting room where the boys were and the whispers as people made small talk, very small talk to break the silence.

Half-way across on that bus journey a prison officer would come in and count the number of people on the bus. Where they thought we might have got out always puzzled me. Why they thought we might want to get out puzzled me even more.

The boys were always in great spirits, whether it was that they put it on so as not to worry us or that they had a great camaraderie there that kept their sanity – probably a bit of both. It was always lovely to see them and if you got that far with the little notes in your mouth, you passed them when you gave them a kiss or under the table, depending on who were visiting. The notes worried me. Carrying them wasn't something I had to do very often so I was not well-practised in the art of carrying them or delivering them. These notes were the only private communication of the prisoners as every letter was censored. They were written on cigarette papers, stuck together, then sealed with Clingfilm and the light of a match.

You were searched both coming into and going out of the prison. Your shoes were taken off and your mouth was checked for these notes and other things. If you were caught carrying anything you would be charged. If you swallowed the note to save yourself from this ordeal, there was always the possibility of being arrested, being brought to a hospital and having your stomach x-rayed to find them.

I had never met Seamus McElwain, who was shot with my brother, but I do remember bringing his sister up with me when I was going to visit Kevin years before. That time she asked me to bring a book in to him for her as she had too many parcels. I had no problem doing this but when the security people saw the name of the book they laughed and sent me straight back to the car with it. It was called *101 Ways of Survival*. This was two months before the big escape in August 1983, when thirty-eight men escaped from the most secure prison in Europe. Seamus led six men to freedom across the fields of Northern Ireland to south of the border.

Kevin was released in 1988 after spending eight years in Long Kesh. Two and a half years later, he was rearrested on the day he was to book his wedding and charged. He was twenty-nine.

I remember that first time I went up to see him in Crumlin Road Jail. He was held like every other person charged with a political offence, without bail, guilty until proven innocent. It was a big, old, ugly prison in a loyalist area in the centre of Belfast and a frightening place. I parked my car in a very open space and crossed the Crumlin Road to stand in the street waiting to get in.

The coldest place on earth, Mammy always said. Apart from the fact that it was not a place you wanted to be, you were left exposed to the elements of both the weather and the war. My car had southern registration plate, which stood out in the North like a sore thumb, and in Belfast, in a loyalist area, it was something else. I hated the place. Bad as the Kesh was, you felt safe enough going there. I could only imagine what this antiquated building looked like inside.

There Kevin was, with the big smile as usual. I said, 'I know you're going to get out, Kevin,' not only because I wanted to make him feel better but because I believed it. 'We can't take much more of this,' I thought. What I meant was, 'I can't take any more of it.'

I always felt guilty about Kevin and it was only recently that I understood why. He was two years younger than me and our job as children was to take care of the ones younger than ourselves. I left home at eighteen when Kevin was sixteen and I think I blamed myself that I did not stay and mind him. He was arrested a year later.

Now he was back in. The next two years were hell, with no one giving him any hope – not the solicitors, the barristers or the family – even though he had lots of witnesses to place him away from the incident he was being charged with. Only I could see him getting out. I remember my elder sister saying, 'You've been too long out of the country, too long to understand.' She didn't want my hopes being dashed and repeated, 'He will not get out.'

During this time I acted as normally as I possibly could in Roscommon: no one knew about my other life or my family. I couldn't tell anyone anything. I had kids at school and I did not want anyone to judge them.

I remember once when someone I knew very well and considered a friend found out what my background was. I was passing her house one day after Christmas and stopped to ask if she had a real Christmas tree, as I would get rid of it for her when I was giving mine to a friend for firewood.

'No,' she said sarcastically, 'we don't kill anything in our house – not even a tree. Do we son?' bringing her young son into the conversation.

How could I possibility explain to this woman that at the same age her son was now I was left with no option but to consider killing. How easy it was for her to make this remark about something she knew nothing about, something I had no choice but to live with.

I remember once Roisín came home from school very excited and said, 'You know, Mammy, there was a man shot at our school one time. He was the teacher and the Black and Tans came in and shot at him and he had to climb out the back window to escape. He was in the IRA, you know, and they were fighting to send the English home.'

I asked, 'Did anyone ask about the IRA today?'

'Seamus asked what was the difference.'

'And what did the master say?'

'He said it wasn't the same.'

I couldn't help myself. I said, 'Will you tell the master from me that if it was all right to kill someone in self-defence in 1921 it's OK today.'

I thought. 'How will I ever be able to tell her that I would have killed? How could she ever understand? How could anyone?'

'Will you tell the master that?'

'No.'

'I will,' said Jarlath, from behind her.

My children knew nothing about my background or that they had two uncles in Long Kesh. I tried not to be bitter but I knew I was, so I told them as little as possible about the Troubles. I didn't want them to have to carry my burden of secrecy.

Years later when Seán was out on day release near the end of his term, I brought them up at home to Fermanagh to see him.

We stood on the front street of my other home and looked out over to the Cuilcagh Mountains that straddled the border. Seán asked, 'Has your man not finished that house yet? He started that before I went to jail.'

I hoped the kids didn't hear but Jarlath, especially, never missed anything. He asked, horrified, 'What was Uncle Seán doing in jail?'

'Well,' said I, very glad I had told them a little, 'remember I told you about political prisoners?'

'Yes.'

'Seán is a political prisoner and is out on day release because he'll be home for good soon.'

'Were any more of my uncles in there?' he asked.

'Yes. Uncle Kevin too, but don't say anything to anyone. Not all your cousins know.'

'Were you ever in there, Mammy?'

'No, pet.'

I knew then I had to tell him something else.

'You know your friend Ciaran? Well his uncle was in with Uncle Seán and they are friends too.' Before this I would watch the two boys play together on the same team, great friends, thinking, isn't it a small world? But I never said a word.

Jarlath's eyes widened as he thought for a while. 'Can Ciaran stay in our house tonight when we get home?'

'Of course he can,' I said and he went back out to play.

Kevin's trial started before a judge with no jury and for one day of it I drove from Roscommon to Belfast. Not because I wanted to be near the place but to support him.

I'll never forget that day: the place was swarming with armed police as they got up and told lie after lie. It was brutal. My heart was broken. I could hardy see Kevin on the stand and I never got to say hello as they whisked him away afterwards. I travelled home along the M1, that long lonely road that I hated because of the years I had spent travelling to and from Long Kesh.

The trial lasted a few weeks and every night of it I phoned my sister, Kevin's girlfriend and his solicitor but they had no hope. I still believed that there was justice somewhere in the universe. After taking to them I would then put the kids to bed, rent a movie and cut myself off from reality, then to a bed where I found little rest.

During this time I was trying to act as normally as I could in front of my kids. At the time, I was organising swimming for the children at school and remember vividly going on the bus to Claremorris pool with another parent and a teacher. Trying to make conversation that day was what sticks in my mind, something that usually comes as naturally to me as breathing. Kevin was on trial and I had to talk about mundane things. My heart was broken with worry and I could say nothing.

The morning of the decision, four or five of the family drove to Belfast. I went to Fermanagh to be with Dad and Mam. I had still not lost hope, not even that morning when I stopped for diesel and a magpie landed on my car. For a moment my heart sank but before I could move a muscle another landed beside it: one for sorrow, two for joy. It was ten thirty.

As I pulled on to the street at home Mammy came running out. 'He's on his way home!' she said. I cried.

Kevin arrived home a few hours later and the house started to fill up with neighbours and friends. Later he pulled me aside in the packed sitting room and said, 'You know you were the only one who ever thought I'd get out.'

As the day worn on, he listened to every news broadcast, on the hour, and said, 'Not a word about my release.'

'Why Kevin, do you not believe you are out?' I asked, bemused.

'No,' he said, 'It's just that, if I was convicted, it would be the headlines on every bulletin.'

Before I left that night I found out that Kevin had been released at ten thirty. I went home and continued chopping wood and drawing water.

13

The Blame Game

The game we play when we don't want to look at ourselves. This is what I did. I lived in a country where everything was censored, including my memories. The media in the Republic was very one-sided and I could not believe what some broadcasters said.

On 20 March 1993 the IRA bombed Warrington in Cheshire and two children were killed. There was uproar everywhere and rightly so. One boy died that day. He was three years old and his name was Jonathan Ball. A second boy, Timothy Parry, died five days later.

It was wrong – so terribly wrong – but I was sickened by everyone signing books of condolences throughout the country and sending planeloads of flowers to England. It took me years to understand what really happened to me at that time.

The day Timothy Parry died, five Catholic workmen were shot by UDA/UFF in their work van in Castlerock, County Derry. Four of these men died. They also had names, which were barely mentioned on the television news or in the papers. I found their names in *Lost Lives*, a book by David McKittrick about all the people killed in the Troubles. These men were twenty-one-year old Noel Kane, twenty-five-year-old James Kelly, fifty-two-year-old James McKenna, father of four children, and Gerry Dalrymple, fifty-eight, father of six. That same day sixteen-year-old Damien Walsh was shot by a UDA/UFF gunman in the Twinbrook estate on the outskirts of West Belfast. He scarcely got a mention either.

I walked the streets of the town I lived in and watched, horrified, as people signed books of condolences for the children killed in Warrington and not a mention of the four dead men in Derry or of the child killed in Belfast. I did not sign the book as I do not believe these children were any more or less important that our fellow countrymen. I remember wondering why I was not strong enough to say anything but that day I was forced back to my childhood when I had no voice. I was now living in a state that was supposed to be free but I was not free to speak.

Damien Walsh's uncle, Dr Seán Loughlin, Associate Professor of Public Administration at Erasmus University in Rotterdam, wrote to *The Irish Times* about the hurt that had been caused by the contrasting reactions to Damien's death and those of the two children killed in Warrington:

> Most people in Northern Ireland, including Damien's family, were profoundly shocked by the Warrington atrocity and the deaths of the two children. Indeed at Damien's funeral Mass prayers were said for the parents and families of the Warrington children. What the family could not understand was why this wave of emotion could not be extended to Damien, who was still only a boy? Damien's family received no planeloads of flowers from the Republic, nor from England. The only cards from the South were from relatives and one Trinity [College] student from Derry.
>
> The purpose of this letter is not to score points but to make a point; every single life is unique and precious. There must be no discrimination in our reactions to murder, which is always the supreme evil. In their understandable reaction to Warrington, people in the South of Ireland should be careful to remember those other dozens of children and young people murdered in the North of Ireland.

I found this letter in *Lost Lives* when I looked for the boy's name and the names of the men killed in Derry.

A few days afterwards the IRA claimed that one of the men killed in Derry was a member of their organisation, Gerry Ryan, one of the top radio presenters in the Republic at that time, commented on his show: 'It's a pity there were not all in the IRA.' I had no choice but to switch off my radio, feeling totally isolated in my own country. Gerry Ryan was probably saying what everyone else was thinking and he was free to say things like this about innocent people.

When I was having flashbacks day after day in 2005 I started
this poem in the middle of a very long, dark night and I finished it
while I was writing this book when I understood better.

> The Media
>
> *We were a bleak reminder or their past,*
> *Their past they wanted to forget,*
> *Their brutal past,*
> *Our brutal present,*
> *They didn't want to know,*
> *They wanted to blame,*
> *They blamed us,*
> *Why?*
> *Why could they just not accept?*
> *Accept what they didn't,*
> *They called it the Troubles,*
> *It was a war,*
> *A brutal war.*
> *Yes, we were a reminder of their past,*
> *Their past they wanted to forget,*
> *Their past which they could not deal with,*
> *Their past that we were a by-product of,*
> *A war,*
> *A civil war.*

At that time I thought I couldn't live in the South any more. I felt
I didn't belong, I didn't belong anywhere. We Northern Catholics
were wanted neither north or south of the border – we who, by
no choice of our own, were left abandoned as a minority in a land
that was divided by others to make peace that we were not part of.
The people here had not dealt with their own past: how could they
possibly deal with our present. But something always kept me from
living in the North. I had a deep-rooted fear that I could not yet
understand.

While editing this book I finally tracked down the front-page
newspaper article that reminded me why I never told my story
to friends or neighbours and why on that day I reinforced the
wall I had built when I was a child. The paper was the *Sunday*

Independent of 28 March 1993. A few lines reported the murders of five Northern Catholics, who were not even given the courtesy of being named (and the number of dead was reported incorrectly). In this article Anne Harris tried to justify why she and others in the South could not express any grief about those killed in the North:

> Of course our grief about Warrington is a sort of a displacement. But in no way is it a misplaced gesture. There is no way the Irish people can express grief about the atrocities in the North any longer.
>
> If we sign books of condolences about the five Catholic workmen murdered in Castlerock, we fear we may be giving succour to the IRA.
>
> And the terrible truth is, a callousing has taken place about the victims of IRA and UFF terror.

Damien Walsh was not even mentioned and the next six pages were filled with commentary about the IRA terror in Warrington.

Maybe if this journalist had to admit to herself and her readers that a sixteen-year-old had been murdered, she would have had to admit that he too was only a boy. She was correct when she said that a callousing had taken place, not on that day but more than twenty-five years earlier when the Troubles started and the minority in the North were left abandoned, no one intervening when they were burnt out of their houses and shot in their farmyards and on the streets because they marched for their civil rights, shot by the people who were there to protect them, victims of state terror.

On 13 June 2010, more than seventeen years after these atrocities, I sat in my home in Roscommon with the pages of the *Sunday Independent* of 28 March 1993 scattered on my sitting room floor as I watched television. At 7.30 one of my favourite programmes, *Reeling in the Years*, began. The year in question that night was 1993 and I cried as all my memories of that time were thrown up again. The Warrington bombings were mentioned and the outcry of the time (with no mention of the men in Derry or the child in Belfast – but how could the person compiling this documentary find this information when it was not available?).

Susan McHugh, a Dublin housewife who started a peace

movement at the time, was shown standing on a podium in Dublin surrounded by 30,000 people. She said, 'I speak for a child when I say, "Please, please, please make it stop."' I could barely breathe as I remembered 1972, when I was one of those children, silently crying for help under my blankets when there was no one listening. It was the year that started with fourteen innocent people killed by British soldiers in Derry. Before the year ended, 495 people were dead. It was a year when a teenager felt such hopelessness that she started to think of ways of protecting herself and her family, a year that ended with her knowing that she could kill if necessary.

1972

> *Adolescence beckoned with great expectations,*
> *Innocence of youth, expectations of the innocent,*
> *365 days, 495 deaths later, it ended,*
> *With the loss of that innocence*
> *And the death of those expectations.*

When the Saville Report on Bloody Sunday was published on 15 June 2010 the British Prime Minister, David Cameron, said, 'On behalf of our country, I am deeply sorry.' I cried again, this time with joy. Before that week was out, I turned fifty-one and could finally let go of the child in me that needed constantly to defend herself by whatever means she felt was necessary.

Reeling in the Years showed the end of the Waco siege and it was only then that I remembered at that time I was in Roscommon hospital on a penicillin drip for three days as I tried to swallow, my throat nearly closed in. This was the start of my illnesses but also the start of my healing, my journey back to heal the forgotten child in me who had had no voice and no help.

I was neither a friend nor relative to any of the five murdered human beings but another Catholic born into the minority north of the border and now trying to hold her own sanity south of the border, where I was part of a majority who accepted me as one of their own religion but not one of them.

As I meditated after writing this, twenty-four women appeared in my recovery room, the wee room inside myself in which I heal, each representing a year I spent living in a county where I was not accepted, a country where I hid who I was and what I had gone through to survive. Today these women return home as I speak on their behalf for the first time, finally free to be themselves.

When the refugees started to flood into Ireland, I heard a dark-skinned well-spoken African woman tell what she had gone through in her own country and how it was for her to live here and as an Irishwoman living in her own land I knew exactly how she felt. It was then I wrote my first poem in years. It was bitter, angry and emotional and I sent it to the *Roscommon Herald*. It was printed in the following week's edition.

> *Refugee*
>
> *Who am I?*
> *I am your neighbour, I am your friend.*
> *I speak the same language as you, I hold the same passport.*
> *Who are you?*
> *You who speak with such authority of things you know nothing*
>   *about.*
> *Who am I?*
> *I am a Northern, I am a nationalist,*
> *I am a person who has had family, friends and neighbours,*
> *Tortured, imprisoned and murdered by foreigners.*
> *And I say 'God help you, refugees, who speak with foreign*
>   *tongues.*
> *This is who I am*
> *Who are you?'*

I put my name and the name of the town I lived under it. Only one person asked me about it. He said 'I know how you feel, my wife has relations in West Belfast.' It was much later that I realised that the reason people in the twenty-six counties did not know what was really going on was because there was censorship of the media that came from a much higher level.

It was only at the final editing of this book that I realised that I still held anger and blame in my heart. I also realised that it was I who was stopping my own healing: you cannot heal fully when you hold any bitterness or anger and when they are removed you are past needing to blame.

The following story is one I have always told to people when they are quick to blame: You are lying peacefully asleep in bed and a child cries. You jump up when you realise the child has fallen out of the cot. What do you do next? Leave it lying there on the floor as you run past it to find someone to blame for leaving the side of the cot insecure? You would never do that, you think, but it's what we do all the time to ourselves. We run past the crying child to find someone else to blame. While we do this we are back to ignoring the wounded child in ourselves.

I had learnt to stop blaming and start healing. There is a saying: to learn, read; to know, write; to master, teach. And I was teaching best what I needed to learn most.

14

Maybe the Worst Thing that Ever Happened to You Will Turn Out to Be the Best Thing that Ever Happened

Back in my other life everything looked perfect. I was a great actress. We bought the house next door to us and I took on another project. As long as my head was full of plans there was no time to think of the thing I had never dealt with.

I oversaw the men who extended the house we had just bought and redecorated it myself. I was a workaholic. I was now working so hard and was so stressed that I was sick most of the time. Not a sickness where I would vomit but a sickness where my stomach always seemed to be full and I could not eat. Ski pants were in fashion at the time and I lived in them. I could wear them with a big jumper and no one could see how swollen my stomach was. I could no longer wear my jeans. I could not bear anything tight around my waist.

I was up early every morning and to bed late at night and it came to the point where all I could eat was rice, yoghurt and pasta because they were bland and did not repeat on me. Going out or away anywhere was becoming a nightmare.

When I went up home Mammy would always have food for me and I could not eat it. I didn't know what to tell her. I could not understand it myself but I knew if my head was full of plans and plenty of work to do I could ignore it. I was like a runaway train. I did not know where to stop and I needed to run faster and faster to keep my mind off this sickness.

One time I was up at home and was so bad I asked Mammy to take me to her doctor. I remember sitting on the side of his couch and saying, 'I would give every penny I own to take the sickness out of my stomach for an hour.' It had taken over my life, it was the only thing I could think of and the only thing that kept it at bay was work.

I remember Marty and I going away on a barge for a few days and I was so sick and did not want to tell him or anyone. I would never vomit, because there was a fear in me of getting sick.

Apart from the six patients I had downstairs I also had a one-bedroom apartment which I had rented, and when the tenant left I had more space. I knocked a wall out, which left me with an extra bedroom, bathroom and sitting room so I took in two more patients and worked even harder. It was becoming more and more difficult to stop. I was on the edge.

It was now 1993, a very difficult year. I was so upset by the state of things at home in the North that I drove to Belfast to see Seán. By this time he was the OC in Long Kesh and I knew if any one knew anything he would. I wanted someone to tell me that this was going to end soon. There were killings on all sides on a regular basis and it was horrific. It reminded me of 1972.

I went up on my own. The kids were too big to bring. They would ask too many questions. Seán was in the waiting room and we chatted about everything but he must have known how worried I was because when I was leaving he said, 'Don't worry Mary, we're talking. It's going to be sorted soon.'

When I told Marty later that night he said, 'You must be joking. They will never sort it out.' But I believed Seán.

Living in a war develops parts of you that most people never need but it leaves undeveloped parts that are essential to survive. I always knew when things were happening. I knew the night that John Major came on TV and said, 'It would make me sick to talk to Gerry Adams,' that he was already talking to him. I remember saying to Marty that night it was on the news, 'He'll phone Gerry Adams after he said that and tell him he had to say this and Gerry Adams will understand, as I understood it.'

'Where do you get those notions?' Marty wondered.

But it was true and I knew it because I was tuned into war and how it worked. You always knew who did what and who was lying. You just knew well. I was rarely wrong.

This came with a big price to me because when I was fine-tuning this awareness to survive I was emotionally immature. I was still a child, a child who never got a chance to develop naturally.

The Troubles raged on and we bought another property. I needed to be busy again. It was taking a terrible toll on my health but at this point I did not know how to stop or, if I did stop, I did not know what else to do so I tore into more work. The people of the town thought I was either mad or the best worker they had ever seen.

I could put on a show as if I was superwoman. I was getting very tired but everything had to keep going. One thing I learned from this time is that if you don't stop when you need to, your body will stop you.

In 1994 the IRA had a ceasefire, a long-awaited ceasefire. Everyone celebrated while I panicked. I panicked because the ceasefire was one-sided and yet again I felt my parents were open targets in a remote house in the countryside in Fermanagh. Seán at this time was spokesman for the political prisoners and very well known. My parent's house would have easily been found or been easy for the police to lead someone to. I went up home and tried to tell Mammy as gently as I could that they would have to be very careful. I had even decided to suggest that moving out for a while might be an option.

Was I paranoid because I was on the edge or had being on the edge so long made me paranoid? Either way I had to say something so I made the journey up home again to talk to her. When I got there she immediately told me that she and Dad were going to America to visit Daddy's sister. She had finally convinced him to get back on a plane and they were to fly out on the day of the ceasefire and would be gone for three weeks.

Three weeks' grace! I was delighted and prayed that the Loyalists would have their ceasefire before they returned. I had watched the war long enough to know that anyone who was going to be taken out would be taken out just before a ceasefire. Old scores would be settled before it was announced on every side.

Brendan was at home at that time and I knew I had only another few weeks to worry. One night I called him and he whispered on the phone, 'I'm under the bed.'

'What's happening?' I asked in a panic.

'All the lights went out in the house when Philly and I were playing cards.'

My heart stopped.

'I'll call you back,' he said and hung up.

Had all my fears been realised? I paced the floor and did not know what to do. What could I do eighty miles away but wait? I have no idea how long I waited until the phone rang again and he said, 'It's okay, Mary. All the lights are out everywhere. We're okay.'

A week later, the Loyalists announced a ceasefire. Mammy and Daddy came home. Everyone celebrated and I switched off the TV. I knew it was now time to sort myself out.

We were bringing the children to Scotland on holiday and I thought the holiday would give me a break. Before leaving, I went to see my doctor, Greg. I laid my head on his table and said, 'I am so tired.'

'You need a good rest,' he said. 'Go home and get someone in to help you.'

'But I'm going to Scotland tomorrow.'

'Don't go.'

I didn't take his advice but was so tired that I stayed in bed in Fermanagh for two days before I could make the rest of the journey. I thought I was better. I was a little better but it was short-lived.

We came home from the holiday and I knew it was time to get professional help so back to Greg I went. I was at crisis point, the point we usually have to get to before we do anything about anything.

It had got to the point that I was barely able to get out of bed in the morning and sometimes went back as soon as the children had gone to school. I was not able to keep up with all the work and sometimes sat staring out the window for hours at a time. It was as if there was so much in my head that I could not get another thing in and I would have to squint my eyes to think.

I told Greg, 'I can't eat right. I go to bed with a sick stomach and I get up with a sick stomach and it's making me so tired.'

I think he knew what was wrong but I insisted that it was all physical. He sent me for all kinds of tests. I had two anaesthetics within two days at two different hospital because you see I had a deadline to sort this out. I always worked with a deadline!

That night in the hospital after the second anaesthetic I thought I would die. I had never been so sick in my life. It was getting to the end of August and the deadline to sort this was before the children went back to school in September. I had to go for one more test and when I went for the results the doctor said there was nothing wrong with my bowel. All the tests had come up clear.

I wanted to have something. I needed a name for this. It had to be labelled and boxed like every thing else in my life. I needed an answer. I asked the specialist. 'Is this all in my head?'

'That is not for me to say,' he replied.

Monica, my friend and neighbour, had brought me to the hospital that day as she had many times before. Her daughter and mine are like sisters. Not a day passed that Monica and I did not talk a few times.

We returned from the hospital in Galway. Roisín stayed with Monica and I went down to make the teas for the patients. Jarlath was out playing with his friends. I was alone in the kitchen and the reality hit me that I had nowhere else to turn. Something broke. I fell to my knees on the kitchen floor and called Monica. 'Bring me to Greg. There is something awfully wrong with me.'

While I was there on the floor crying, the phone rang and I really don't know why I answered. Geraldine said hello and heard me crying. She said, 'What is wrong with you?' and from somewhere deep inside me I answered, 'I don't know but this all has to do with the North.'

Greg had humoured me, sending me for all the tests, when he knew I was heading down the slippery slope of depression and my sickness had nothing to do with my stomach. He was a very shrewd man, who knew that a diagnosis was not always made on what was visible to the eye. He lived on the same road as me and would have had a good idea of my background as his wife was from the same county. He has such a good way with people and would have you laughing every time you went in to him, if there was a smile anywhere in you.

I already had a good relationship with him. He was the doctor to most of my patients and I could call him at any time if I had any problems with them. He could not pass my house on his nightly walk but one of them would wait in the shadows and stop him if he had any ailment at all. Greg would listen patiently and then say, 'Frank, you come down to see tomorrow morning in the surgery and I'll take care of you.' Frank would then come to my door and tell me excitedly that he was wanted in the surgery in the morning.

I remember a few times when he left me in stitches laughing. Once he asked Roisín, while she trembled at the thought of the needle that was coming, 'What are you going to be when you grow up, Roisín?'

'A doctor like you,' she replied without hesitation (you always wanted to be like someone you liked and Roisín liked Greg).

'Ah, Roisín,' he said, 'don't be. Be a dentist. They'll not be calling you out at night.' And Roisín laughed as the needle went into her arm.

He also told me that the night he sent me back to the hospital for the second time before Jarlath was born he called to ask how I was. 'By the looks of her,' said my favourite nurse, 'she is not in labour.'

'Well,' said Greg, 'it was the first time I've ever heard that you could tell by the look of someone.'

Now I was back to him with not a smile on either of our faces as we both knew I had a serious problem. 'You're depressed, Mary, and this is the best thing that has ever happened to you.'

I could not believe what he said: this man whom I trusted was telling me that this was the best thing that had ever happened to me. Years later I agreed with him. It *was* the best thing that ever happened to me. My body stopped me with something I could survive.

15

Facing the Truth
and the Long Road Home

'You are depressed, Mary,' Greg said with the most sombre face I had ever seen on him. 'Will you go to see a psychiatrist?'

'Yes,' I replied, without hesitation.

He mentioned a local doctor and I said, 'No I can't go there,' because this person was the psychiatrist to most of my patients and I could not afford to lose them because I was depressed – not only because it was my living but also because they were, at this point, minding me. They seemed to understand better than even I did. They knew because they were seeing someone going through the same thing they had.

He mentioned another name and it rang a bell somewhere in me. I had not heard the name in years but when he said Delia McGuinness I asked if she was from Fermanagh. She had gone to primary school with my brother and sister. How I remembered that I have no idea but something was working with me now that I was on the right road.

He gave me a prescription and said he would make an appointment for me with Delia and as I walked out the door he said, 'Mary, go out and walk every day. It will do you good.'

'I don't have the time.'

'Make the time!' he insisted.

I got the tablets and that night Monica and I went out in the pouring rain for my first walk, a habit I have continued to this day, mostly alone now.

By this time Monica knew a little about our family. It was a long time later before I would tell anyone what happened to me because I was so badly damaged that I trusted no one. She later told me that the night of my first walk she was getting calls from all over the world from my siblings to see what was wrong with me and how I was. We were like sisters at the time and they knew that she would know. She has a great sense of humour and said, 'God, your ones must have been sending out smoke signals, as my phone never stopped ringing all night.'

Our family had become very close because of the war and we were always there for one another, although we might not see one another that often. By this time the family were in London, New York, Australia and God knows where Lucy might have been, probably Nepal around then.

After that first night Monica, Teresa (another neighbour) and I would go walking most mornings. They would chat away and I would listen. The only thing on my mind was how I would get one foot in front of another.

I remember a long time later telling Geraldine that depression is like your body deciding to switch off automatic pilot and go into manual mode. Everything had to be thought out, like walking. 'I will now lift one leg. Now I will lift the other.' This did not leave you in any position to hold a conversation. So Monica and Teresa talked. I listened and I walked.

I hated meeting anyone. I did not know how to cope with doing nothing. Standing there I would just pray it would not be a long conversation but it usually was as both Monica and Teresa were just like me: they loved a good chat. I would be stepping from one foot to the other. They must have thought I was half-mad – and they were probably right – but I was grateful for those walks because home was a nightmare. There was so much to do.

I had help in but there are ways you like things done and the only person who could do a job the way I liked was Roisín, probably because I trained her.

I'd often say to women who came in to help me, 'This is the way I like it done.'

'But this is the way I do it,' would be the reply most of the time and I'd feel like screaming, 'I'm paying you do it the way I want.'

Of course there was nothing wrong with how things were done. I was just stuck in my ways back then. Now as long as it's done I didn't care!

These women were only in a few hours to clean and when I got back home every thing had to be done in manual mode – every task painstakingly thought out – and I dreaded it.

I remember once standing talking with Monica outside her house when I was a lot better. I did not want to go home because I hated to be alone. I was starting to remember things that I did not want to remember.

Slowly walking down the road after I left her, I entered my house as if I was going into a prison – and not for a visit. The post had been delivered and I recognised Seán's handwriting and the Maze stamp on it. I open it and found a card, a pink card with a bunch of flowers on it (too big to be passed through the usual channels so it had censored stamped on it) and on it he had written, 'You are a strong woman, Mary, and you can get through this. I know you can and so do you.'

I cried and I didn't even mind that the prison had stamped HMP Maze Letter Censor, Point No. 4 on it. I could not show it to anyone but I had it and I knew they were all willing me to get better.

The prisoners at this point were making things in the workshop and we would get presents like harps or wee cottages or the picture, done by a neighbour on Perspex, of a old man playing the harp in gold with a sunset behind him. It is beautiful and I still have it on my wall. I hung it up when I got it and I don't think anyone even noticed H-Blocks, Long Kesh, on the bottom of it. If they did they never said. The only comment was, 'That is beautiful.'

Geraldine made a joke one time after the peace agreement: 'We can now take the harps out of the attic.' Mammy could not understand why we did not have them in the middle of the sitting-room coffee table, polishing them every day.

Seán's card reminded me of the card that was also censored on 27 November 1987: a pink baby card (for Roisín) signed by all the fifty men in H Block 2.

Now that my body knew I had started a process, it was not going to let me off the hook. I did not sleep the night I got the tablets or the next and by the third I was back with Greg, who give me different ones.

Mammy and Daddy were down with me at this time as with Marty gone all day I could not cope on my own. I took the new tablets and was asleep in a few minutes but an hour later I was awake again. I walked up and down the corridor in a panic, as the thought of lying awake for another night was more than I could bear. I eventually went into Mammy to get her to bring me to the doctor.

It was midnight when I phoned the doctor on call and told her my story. She said, 'Come up to see me.' I did and she gave me a injection.

I did not even ask what it was; only how long it would take me to get to sleep.

She said twenty minutes. I ran out to the car and said, 'Get me home, Mammy. I'll be asleep in twenty minutes.'

Five hours later I was still awake, sitting up with my knees to my chest and shaking. I called the doctor again.

'Are you still awake?' she asked in amazement.

'What did you give me?'

'I injected you with 30 milligrams of Valium. It would knock out a horse.'

She told me to take another one of the tablets I had and when I did I thought every thing had gone in my head. All I could see were flashes like a fuse box blowing up but it knocked me out for the few hours until morning.

At 9.30, the phone rang. It was Greg. 'I heard you were on the prowl last night,' he said, and I could imagine his smile.

'I just phoned Delia,' he continued, 'and she has changed your appointment to tomorrow, I told her it was an emergency.'

That had to be one of the longest days of my life. Mammy fussed around the house and Dad, as usual, was in the garden. Mammy was in the kitchen baking one cake of bread after another. I sat in the front room, staring into the fire. It felt like something in me had died. I had lost control of everything. That day, I handed it all over to something greater than me as I started my long road home.

Next day Mammy drove me down to Delia through the back roads of Mayo. I was not capable of driving. It was a long journey but I was glad I was going somewhere for help. I knew I was only barely existing.

We waited in her small waiting room, just the two of us and not a word spoken, I found it an effort even to make conversation and I'm quite sure Mammy was just as glad to be there as me.

Delia was not much older than me but seemed a lot older when we were children when one year makes a big difference and three makes an enormous one.

I had never talked to her but it was an unusual name at the time we were children and it always stuck in my mind.

'How do you feel?' she asked.

I explained what was happening with me and then asked, 'Are you from Lisnaskea?'

'Yes.'

'I am too,' I said, before she could say another word.

'Who are you?'

'Mary Lynch. You went to school with my sister Geraldine.'

'Are you PJ's sister?'

'Yes.'

She put down her pen and notebook, leaned back in her chair and said, 'How is your mother? I have often wondered how she coped.'

'She's in the waiting room and a lot better than me.'

She continued to question me and I remember she asked, 'Do you think you are fat?'

'No, Delia,' I answered as I looked down at my body that was wasting away. 'I am like a rake and I am not anorexic, I would give anything to be able to eat and put on at least a stone and look normal.'

A few weeks before, Monica and I had decided to bring the children swimming. It was probably her idea to get me out of the house. I went with her but when I had tried on my swimming suit I would not go into the water looking like I did.

Delia was great. Before I left she give me both her home number and that of her holiday home and told me to call if I ever needed her. It was the security I needed. I did call once; maybe that was just to check she was really there.

She promised me that I would not get addicted to the Valium she prescribed, as I was afraid I would, because it was only short-term and she would have me off it very quickly. She then explained why I needed it now.

We stopped off at a chemist on the way at home as I knew every pharmacist in my town and did not want anyone to know I was on Valium and anti-depressants. I asked the pharmacist to put the tablets in half the prescription dose so I would not have to use as strong a dose and sometimes I even split these. I had by then been working with psychiatric patients for a long time and knew how addictive this medication was and how more and more became necessary to get the same results.

After a month on the anti-depressant medication I slowly found myself coming back to some semblance of normality. Delia had said it was just a chance to give myself a rest. 'I'll then take you off everything gradually after six months.' But as I improved I thought I could stay on these for the rest of my life. This was dependency but the alternative was not something I wanted to think of right now.

Geraldine called me every night; I remember her asking me one night, as she always did, 'How are you tonight?'

I said, 'A lot better than last night. It's a good job you didn't call me then.'

'I did! I was talking to you last night, Mary.'

I had no memory of it.

Mammy took me home for a week and Marty took over the patients and children. Mammy played bowls at that time and went out the next night to play. Dad had gone visiting so I was alone in the house. I was petrified to be alone but Ruth was going to call. She did and left me ten minutes before Mam came back. It was the longest ten minutes of my life. It was as if I was afraid of myself. I was afraid of what I had to remember.

When I went back home Ruth came with me and stayed a week and then it was Gertie's turn. All the orders for support were probably coming from Mammy – not that the girls would have minded, as we had got our sense from children that our job was to take care of one another.

Ruth was brilliant. She would relieve us every year when we went on holidays when Mam and Dad couldn't make it and all the patients loved her. She knew exactly what to do so I could rest. All my friends and most of the shopkeepers in the town knew her too because she would be doing all the buying when I was gone – and there was a lot of buying for us and our extended family.

Years later she ran for Sinn Féin as a county councillor. I was so excited when she won by a landslide. I told someone I knew and was surprised when her first question was, 'What party did she run for?'

When I said Sinn Féin she replied with the most puzzled expression, 'But Ruth is a lovely girl!'

I replied, 'She is still a lovely girl.'

The government and the media had done a great job here to demonise Sinn Féin with their Section 31, whereby no member of the party could speak on the TV or radio without a voice-over. She couldn't believe that Ruth was a member of this party. My American friends used to laugh at the idea that people's voices could not be heard as someone spoke their words beside them – as if they were speaking a foreign language.

I remember Ruth telling me once that she had more problems with the fact that she was a woman than with the fact that she was in Sinn Féin. She was the only woman member of the county council at the time, along with twenty-two men.

Next came Gertie, who is the complete opposite to Ruth. She's a real gentle soul, nearly ten years younger than me. When Mammy brought her home from the hospital I thought she was the most beautiful wee thing I had ever seen with her golden hair and blue eyes. I wondered if Mammy had run out of colour. After eleven children, she could not have much colour left for Gertie.

We had black, brown, strawberry blondes and dirty blondes in the family and now this little girl arrives with golden hair. I would brush that hair and keep her clean. She was my little doll – dolls were in very short supply; in fact I don't ever remember having one. Santa always brought Lego and games. That might be the reason most of the boys worked in construction and I love building and renovating houses!

Gertie stayed a week and we both sat and rested. She is the type of person who would make you just feel better because she slowed you down. When she left on the Sunday evening I said to her, 'How am I going to cope on my own?' Years later she told me she did not understand but cried all the way back to Dublin The six months passed in a haze. I was coping and the prescriptions were finished. I went back to Delia for what I thought was the last time.

16

BACK TO THE BEGINNING

When I first finished the medication I asked Delia how bad I was. 'On a scale of one to ten with ten being the worst,' she said, 'I would have put you at a nine and a half.'

Back home I felt myself go down again rapidly. I couldn't cope without the drugs and for the first time in my life I understood why people stayed on them for so long. You are not better but it takes the edge off the pain and saves you from looking at the source of the problem.

I did not know what to do. I was supposed to be better but I was getting worse by the day. I was sinking back into a black hole of despair.

It got to the point that one day I found myself in the graveyard picking a plot where I would like to be buried. I was looking for a big tree where I would be protected.

'Did you think you were going to kill yourself?' my sister asked later.

'No. I didn't need to. I was already dead.' That exactly how I felt, as if I was completely dead. Nothing was working. I had no feelings about anything. It was as if I was a zombie.

When I met Delia again she said, 'Mary, whatever is wrong in your life get it sorted. You don't want to be on these tablets for the rest of your life.'

I said, 'I feel I have been silenced for so long. I have never have been able to tell anyone who I really am. I don't even know myself any more.'

'I can understand why you could not tell anyone about your family,' Delia continued. She understood this well as a northerner living south of the border. I had known this for a very long time and understood the untold damage the silence had done to me. They say silence is golden; it is unless it is forced.

Delia gave me a three months' prescription and I was left to stop and take a long hard look at my life.

The time frame in total was six months. Six months to get myself together and that was that. I knew she was right.

I started to go line dancing with two friends every week. This was great therapy for me. I had always loved to dance. I was also walking.

My business had to be kept going and I needed to employ someone to help. But no more property developing.

I did all this but as the day approached to give up the medication I drove to Enniskillen and got myself a supply of St John's Wort, a natural antidepressant which was banned in the health food shops in the Republic. I was still frightened to go it alone.

I started on St John's Wort the day I finished the prescription drugs. About this time I also started looking at alternative practices. My friend Mary had started to do a massage course and had been using me as one of her case studies. I loved it and continued to go to her when she qualified.

Then another friend Maura decided to do reflexology and also used me as a case study. The reflexology and massage relaxed me so much that I was starting to remember things from my past.

I needed a break to get away from everything so when Brendie decided to get married in New York, I flew back to the Big Apple where a lot of family and friends of both Brendie and Jenny had arrived for the wedding.

Mammy travelled from the North with my sisters and we all met in Lucy's apartment in Brooklyn for a week together. Mammy was watching me like a hawk and I was trying to stay as positive as I possibly could. It was a good week and I returned home with six months' supply of my natural drug, as it was much cheaper there.

When I came home again I wanted more help from Marty, which was not forthcoming. I needed help in the house with both patients and children, but by this time he had his six and a half days on the farm and was not going to give them up.

Farming, I have always maintained, is a rich man's hobby and whatever was being made was being pumped back into it. Marty was a great worker and great farmer but things were at crisis point in the house and I was not able to hold everything together on my own. I knew this and had started to demand more of him.

This is when I had my first thought of counselling. I said to him, 'We need to go for counselling. We need help to talk to each other.'

I was well aware of the consequences if I maintained my workload. My meditation, which I diligently maintained twice a day, and a little yoga every morning were keeping me sane. I had started them both in New York when I first went there: yoga to help my back, with which I had a lot of problems and meditation for my mind. Marty had been practising this for a long time before I met him.

I changed my walking pattern around this time and started walking an hour every day when the kids were at school; around back roads so the only people I met would be the odd farmer. This hour give me the time to think and talk to myself.

Looking up to the heavens one day I said, 'I need help. I will do whatever is necessary to get my life back on track. I will let my marriage go if necessary. I will even let my children go to Marty if I need to but please allow me to keep my children if I possibly can. I cannot go on like this or I will be no good to anyone, least of all myself.'

I was on the slippery slope again. I think this was second time in my life that I asked for help, the first being when I went to Germany alone. It is also when I learnt that you have to let go of everything in order to move on. No such thing as, 'I'll hold on to this or that.' When I let it all go, it was then that I was guided.

That night I mentioned marriage counselling to Marty when he returned from the farm but he refused to go.

Okay, I thought, maybe if we had somewhere to get away from all the work at home we could have time together. I suggested that we look for a little holiday home and pay someone to take over in the house when we were gone. I knew we could afford to do this and I also knew we could not afford not to if there was to be any hope for us.

Marty agree to look with me so with Dad and Mam down we took off one morning and headed to Ballina. Marty wanted to go towards Westport where we had often rented a mobile from my friend but I knew we could not afford that area either in price or the time to get there. I figured that if we were to get a place within an hour from our home we would go there.

We had a lovely day, as we usually did when we were away from it all. I drove and Marty directed me up and down back roads. We had lunch in Ballina, having seen nothing, then headed off to Enniscrone, a beautiful little village on the coast, but it was not what I wanted. Too many people there. Peace and quiet is what we both had in mind. Heading home on our first day out looking we were not at all disappointed and again took all the back roads.

We were passing a beautiful lake when Marty said, 'I think we were here this morning. Take the next right.' There in the shadow of the Ox Mountains was a little cottage for sale. All my life I had lived by my gut feeling and my gut loved this place. I knew instantly this is what I was looking for and Marty agreed. There was a peace in the air that I could not describe. We walked around the cottage. It would need to be gutted but that did not faze me. I knew this was right and that we could have a place to hide in and chill out.

We took the number of the auctioneer and crossed the road to a small bungalow to get more information. A woman with a big smile opened the door. She was a few years older than myself and introduced herself as Mary. I enquired who owned the house and she said her it was her mother's and took me in to meet her mother, Mamie. She then took us back across to the cottage and showed us inside and told us the price.

I told her we might be interested and said we'd see them again when we talked to the auctioneer. Getting back into the car I knew it was right and the price was reasonable so we called into the auctioneer on the way back. He tried to sell us something else. We agreed to look but knew right away that we had what we wanted in the first cottage. I was happy as we drove back that evening. We now had a place that would be ours, a place that did not have to have a financial return for its existence.

Negotiations started with both the owners and the county council, as it had no septic tank. I had a home in mind and a place where we could all be together but Marty was having second thoughts. After getting this far I was not letting go. He said, 'Why don't you go back on the tablets and all will be fine?'

Technically he was right but if I needed tablets to save my marriage, I did not need the marriage. I needed to save myself.

We went on holidays to Wicklow that year and it was the worst week we had ever been away together. We had always had great times when we were away from work and in the end I said, 'Either we get help to sort this or we finish it, I cannot live like this any longer.'

Marty agreed because he knew I meant it. He wanted a man as the counsellor and insisted that we go a long way from home. I didn't care where we went or who would guide us – I just wanted help for both of us. This was no atmosphere for children to live in. I had been brought up in a home where my parents showed us a great example of what a good relationship was and I knew it was possible. With the help of the Yellow Pages I went to work and found a place far enough away with a man as the marriage counsellor.

It is a very difficult thing to have to face the reality that your marriage is breaking down, but the alternative seemed to me to be much worse. I had those dark sleepless nights, the medication to which I had no intentions of returning. I did not know where else to go: I had asked the world for help and was following the direction that felt right. I was so looking forward to getting help. I wanted my marriage to work but it was such a struggle to get this far. I was afraid we might not get to the day of the counselling but it eventually arrived. The tension was terrible as we made our way for help in silence, and after an hour of hostile negotiations I endured another silent journey on the way home.

17

Go with that Flow

That night I had promised a friend I would start a Tai Chi class with her, a class that she had organised. She needed people to get it off the ground.

I had no idea what Tai Chi was but went to support her. Maura and her family were very good to me at that time; it was one of the few places that I was free to speak about the things I remembered of my childhood in the North. I had started to tell her these things as they surfaced when she was doing reflexology on me.

John, her husband, was a local schoolteacher, writer and poet. We'd sit in front of their open fire and the three of us would talk. Well, I talked the most and they would listen with interest and I loved them both.

Maura wanted me there early to introduce me to the teacher before anyone else arrived. If I thought I had a bad day that night was to be a shocking one for me. When I arrived, a little late, Maura was already there with a man and a teenage boy who, I later found out, was his son.

Maura said, 'Hi, Mary, this is Dave.'

He put out his hand and said, 'Hi, Mary, Nice to meet you.'

I nearly puked. He was English!

The only conversations I had ever had with Englishmen were forced as they pointed guns at me. I was now having my first memories of my teenage years and the last thing I needed after the day I had was to be confronted by an Englishman who looked like a soldier.

I smiled as best I could and shook his hand, thinking, 'I don't need this and as much as I love you, Maura, I will not be coming back after tonight.' But I felt I had no choice but to go in.

Not only was Dave English but he was arrogant: he stood at the front of the class and explained what Tai Chi was and how it could make you mentally, physically and emotionally stronger.

I don't think many people will understand what happened over the next hour. It was crazy. It was as if something in me went out to meet something in him. It was as if a part of me reached out to meet a long-lost friend. It was as if I had just met someone I knew, whom I had always known. Behind that arrogant façade was someone I recognised.

I was even more stomached when the wee voice in my head, which had for years guided me through my business affairs, was now interfering in my private life. It said to me, 'You can trust him. He will help you and you will help him.'

I was horrified. I trusted no one.

The next morning I went down to my friend Teresa who lived in one of the flats I was renting. We had become great friends when she moved in with her two children after she separated.

To this day I remember what I told her. She was the only one I could tell. I said, 'Teresa, last night I meet a man I have never seen before in my life, but I know that I know him.'

'What do you mean you know him if you don't know him?'

'I don't know what I mean. All I know is that I've never seen him before in my life but it was like I walked in and met a long-lost friend.'

'That's crazy!'

'I know! And what's more, he is everything I don't like.'

I had heard of reincarnation but I never entertained the notion, but right from the beginning I knew Dave and I had travelled on another journey together. The following week I was back at class, amazed at this connection. It was as if there were two levels of him; the human level that I was finding hard to tolerate and another level that I could not walk away from.

I continued the class and looked forward to seeing him. Meanwhile the marriage counselling continued and took a turn for the better.

Every Wednesday morning I went down to Teresa to report what had happened the night before. By this time she had begun to understand on some level and one morning she said, 'Phone him and tell him what you told me.'

'How could I? He'll think I'm crazy!'

'You'll have to, or you'll drive yourself crazy.'

I knew she was right but this notion of reincarnation was foreign to my upbringing and how could it be an English person? I think I could have accepted it more quickly if he had been of any other nationality.

One day soon after I took up the phone and called his number. 'This is Mary from your Tai Chi class. I would like to talk to you about something.'

'About what?'

'Well,' I thought, 'Here goes...'

'I feel as if I know you, as if I have always known you and yet I have never seen you before.'

There was a silence, a long silence, and then he said, 'You had better come down to see me. We need to talk.'

The next day I called to the house that he shared with his wife and two children. He sat at one side of the kitchen and I sat at the other. 'Explain to me what you mean,' he said.

'Well the first night I met you I felt a connection between us, a connection that I don't understand. On a human level I know I don't know you but on another level I seem to know you. I know you can help me and what is more, I know that you need my help. For what I have no idea, but I know you do.'

He was silent for a while and then he said, 'I understand, Mary. You and I have travelled together before.'

Relief flooded through me. I was not crazy. 'Did you know that first time we met? I asked.

'No, but I knew within the first few weeks.'

We talked a little more and when I left, I was satisfied that it was not abnormal. I knew the help I needed and wondered what help I would give him. I later realised that nothing works just one way, even with therapists; they receive as much help from their clients as they give.

The classes continued and I can't say I was mad about his human front but I tolerated it. One night when he was looking for a guinea pig for shiatsu, I lay on the floor in front of him and he worked on me while the rest of the class worked on one another. When the class was over he continued to work on me and when he had finished he sat up with his back against the wall and said, 'What is wrong with you?'

'Why?' I snapped back, 'what do you see wrong with me?'

'There are parts of you ice-cold, parts of you where there is no energy.'

I looked him straight in the eye and made a decision to tell him. 'I have just come out of a depression,'

'What happened to you?'

'People like you is what happened to me.'

'What do you mean "people like me"?'

'Englishmen. British soldiers carrying guns. I'm from the North and our lives and homes were invaded by soldiers and still are up there.'

He thought for a moment and then said, 'If you ever need anyone to talk to, you can talk to me.'

I got up and left thinking, 'If I ever get the courage to talk, it will certainly not be to you or any one like you.'

The classes continued and the bond between us grew on a deep level of understanding. He was a hill-walker and leader and ran a club, which he invited us to join.

'Why don't you?' Teresa said, 'it would get you out of the house and away from work and do you good.'

'What if he brings a gun?' I replied, without thinking.

'What do you mean?'

I had no idea what I meant but I could not believe that he was English and did not carry a gun. It was as if an undeveloped child in me was speaking through me, a child who could not trust him.

A few months later I did go hill-walking and from that first day I loved it. I loved the freedom of the mountains, the fresh air, the exercise, the views. I was hooked. The added bonus was that for the few days after a walk in the mountains, it was as if I was on a drug. I had a natural high.

The cottage we had bought the year before had finally got planning permission but this time I had hired a contractor so that I would not have as much to do. Because the cottage was old I wanted to retain its original features. I wanted to replace any that had been destroyed so I spent any spare time I had running around the country picking up doors, finding recycled slates and all the extras. It was a labour of love and it showed in the house. Marty was no longer interested so I was on my own.

The cottage was at the foot of the Ox Mountains, which I had not even noticed when buying it as I had never considered walking then. Now I could head into the mountains alone and I loved that. I could talk to the mountains and leave a lot of my fears and tears there.

The marriage counselling had finished and for a while I thought Marty and I could work it out but he was back farming all the time and the fragile marriage was crumbling.

I had a grip on the depression and was no longer on any medication, either chemical or natural, but I needed to know what had happened to me as I had a deep-rooted fear that it would happen again.

I made an appointment to see a psychotherapist I had met at a lecture he was giving locally. I drove for more than an hour and a half to get to him but I liked him and I did not care about the long journey. The first day I spoke to him about my background and I cried as I told him I was afraid of slipping back into that black hole.

Half way thought the second appointment he said to me, 'Did anyone ever tell you what you have been suffering from?'

'Yes. Depression.'

'Did anyone explain what type of depression you had?'

'What do you mean?'

'You are suffering from post-traumatic stress.'

I laughed.

'Why do you laugh?' he asked.

'For two reasons. One, because I've always known this; and two, because my sister will say, "Why you? Why aren't we all suffering from it?"'

'Because,' he said, 'it's post with you. They are all still living in it.'

'Mary,' he continued, 'when something traumatic happens to you and you cannot deal with it you shut it off to be dealt with when you are strong enough. You have had nearly thirty years of trauma and you are now strong enough to deal with it.'

It was that simple. After years of trying to figure out what was wrong with me, this man had summed it up in two minutes. I could have hugged him.

Post-traumatic stress: I now had a name after having every test done on my body. There were times when I did not care if they called it cancer as long as it had a name. It had to be labelled to be accepted. Depression is that lonely disease of the body where there are no outward signs, only inward misery – a disease that you cannot understand unless you have experienced it.

I drove home that evening happier than I had been in a long time. I knew what was wrong with me; now all I had to do was to learn to deal with it and make sure it didn't happen again.

18

REMEMBER: SOMETIMES COMFORT CAN BE FOUND IN THE SIMPLEST OF THINGS

I continued to go to Tai Chi and found I was getting stronger and stronger in myself, not only physically but emotionally.

I was now able to hold my own with people I would have let walk over me in the past. People thought I was very strong but they were wrong. I had a very strong exterior but I was soft as butter in the centre. Like the egg: a very hard shell with a very soft yolk. That was the wall I had built to protect myself, like so many other people. The Tai Chi was strengthening the centre and relaxing the outer hard core.

At the time there was an advertisement on TV for toilet roll and I loved it. It said, 'This toilet tissue is soft and strong.' This was how I saw myself in the future: soft and strong. I had been hard and strong. Hard things break, soft things bend. I broke.

One night I dreamt I was standing at a gate and there was a shell falling around me, like plaster of Paris. I told Teresa that this was the wall coming down – a wall that took years to dismantle, as each brick had to be removed with care.

I have had very strange dreams in the past, which were making much more sense to me now. One recurring dream was of being in the chapel and it was time to go for Holy Communion. Everyone was getting up and going to the altar but I could not walk. I would get out of the seat on my hands and knees and crawl to the altar. Nobody noticed. I had been on my hands and knees in reality and nobody noticed, not even myself.

Another dream that was a frequent visitor was one in which I was trying to get from one window to another on the outside of a building, always afraid I was going to fall. But the most frightening dream of all was the one in which I would wake up and could not open my eyes or move a muscle in my body.

Maura and I decided to go to a course in detaching. One night the teacher guided us into a meditation. She told us to visualise ourselves in a room which was full of light and love and where no one could harm us. I found this no problem to do as it was what I had been doing for years.

'Now,' she said, 'there is a door in this room and you can allow anyone in. Anyone. But they cannot harm you. Just relax and see who will come in.'

I was so sure it would be Marty but in walked a British soldier! He came and sat in a chair opposite me.

The teacher continued, 'I want you now to feel relaxed in the presence of this person.' Then she guided us out of the meditation. She went around everyone in the circle and asked each person to tell, if they wished, who had come into the room. When she came to me I did not hesitate to say it was a British soldier, even though it was not something I had ever spoken about before in such a public place.

'What was he doing there?' she asked.

'I'd like to ask him the same question!' I replied.

'When you go home, write to him.'

'But I don't know his name.'

'Just write, "Dear soldier," and see what happens.'

Later that night when everyone else was asleep I sat at the kitchen table and wrote, 'Dear soldier'. I looked around to check that nobody was watching, because I had no idea what I was at.

I didn't know what to write next except, 'What were you doing in my room?'

And then I could not stop writing. By the time I got to the sixteenth page my hand and body were shaking and there was an anger in me that I had never felt before. The anger then made me scribble out the pages until I had nearly ripped them asunder and I was exhausted.

Laying my head on the table I cried and cried, as I tried to speak to him and tell him how he had affected my whole life. It was the first of many pages of writing I would do over the years to come – pages that would take the fears from my body on to the paper, where I could try to understand where they had originated.

The next week in the classroom the teacher asked if I had

written to him. When I told her I had she asked, 'How did you feel afterwards?'

'I felt as if I had opened a file that I had locked in my head for a long time and it was a very healing experience, but does this mean that I have to write to each of the hundreds of other soldiers who passed through my life?'

'No,' she answered, 'the one will do.'

I was still watching Dave but I could not bring myself to trust him. All my life I had listened and trusted my wee voice when it guided me in my business dealings and I had not made many wrong moves but this was different. I had never heard it in my private life before and was finding it difficult to accept that he could be trusted. How could he be? He was one of them.

The foot and mouth disease was keeping us off the mountains and the holiday cottage was finished. I had spent every penny I had, sold every share I had acquired over the years and borrowed the rest from the bank. Now I was stony broke but this had never bothered me before and it did not bother me now, apart from the fact that we could not afford to go anywhere on holidays.

I called Geraldine and asked if we could use her parents-in-law's holiday home in Donegal for a week if no one else was there. She got back to me and said, no problem, we could have it.

I know we had our own holiday home now but after all the work I had put into finishing it, I needed to get away from it all.

It was a very difficult week between Marty and myself and we spoke barely a word on the way home. We arrived back on the Friday and later that night Dave rang. 'Back to the mountains on Sunday. Do you want to come?'

'Brilliant! I'm coming.'

The following morning I had to go to Foxford and was home about five. When I came in I noticed there were three missed calls from my sister and two from home and I knew there was something terribly wrong. In all the years of the Troubles no one had rung more than once. They would wait for you to return the call.

Daddy was over eighty at this time so I feared it was him. I rang Geraldine's number and she said, 'Have you heard about Gary?'

'What about Gary?' I asked (he was our eldest nephew).

'He was killed this morning on his motorbike in New York.'

I could not believe it. He was only twenty-three with everything to live for. We had spent nearly thirty years thinking all of us would never survive the Troubles and now, when they were over, Gary was killed.

I sat on the floor and cried and cried. It was as if a dam had burst in me. Later that night I called Dave and told him. 'Maybe you should just get out in the mountains tomorrow,' he said, 'but you'll know what to do.'

Next morning after a sleepless night I went into Roisín's bedroom and said, 'I'm going out walking. If Nana calls tell I've gone for a walk but don't tell her it's in Sligo.'

There was nothing I could do and I needed to be away for a while.

I walked along in silence while everyone else was chatting. I made a decision; I could no longer live in a marriage that was not working, Gary was only twenty-three and did not have a chance; I was twenty years older and needed to move on.

Gary was born the year before I went to Germany and I had not been around much when he was growing up so I did not know him that well but I knew one thing: that day before I left the mountain, he was beside me.

The body was not brought home for a week and it was the longest week. I would not go home, as there was no point. I arrived after the body. He was buried a few days later, just before 9/11, and we were so grateful to have a body as he worked in that area of New York.

Back at home in Roscommon I continued to cry and cry. They were tears for myself as well as for Gary: tears for a lost life. With the tears, the flashbacks came. All hell had broken loose in my body.

I woke one Sunday morning petrified and crying. I crawled out of bed into the kitchen and under the counter top. I watched as a movie was played in my head, a movie of something I had long forgotten. I was on my knees. I held my head in my hands and could not stop the film that insisted on playing. I had neither the strength nor the desire to hold on to it any longer. All I could see was that gun; that gun pointed at my head as the soldier screamed, 'Get out of your bed!'

I was no longer in my kitchen in the peace of the west. I was a child in bed and a soldier had a gun at my head. It was in freeze-frame and would not move on. I could not move it and I lay down there with no idea what was happening. How long I lay I have no idea but I was frozen when I eventually moved, frozen in both my body and mind. I didn't know what to do. I could not tell Marty as we were barely on speaking terms and I could not tell the children.

A neighbour, Catherine, was picking me up to go walking, I dressed as best I could and went out to meet her. I told her when I got to the car; not that I expected her to understand but I needed to tell someone.

Walking like a zombie up that first steep incline I thought I'd never make it through the day but I knew I was among friends, even if they had no idea what was going on in my head. At lunch Catherine gave me a sandwich, as I had brought nothing with me. I ate it to keep up my strength but with no taste for anything.

When we finished walking that day I don't think I felt any better but I was able to talk. As usual on the way home, we headed to a café, this time in Sligo. 'What would you like Mary?' Catherine asked.

I had avoided chocolate for years now as my diet had to be so bland but today I needed something sweet. My wee voice inside said hot chocolate and I voiced the desire. I will never forget that big mug with its wide brim, full of hot chocolate, covered in fresh cream and sprinkled with chocolate flakes. It was the best thing I had ever tasted and hot chocolate would become my comfort food over the next few years as the flashbacks continued.

19

Healing Begins
when You Start to Face the Truth

Christmas approached and the crying continued. I couldn't stop. I told the children I was crying for Gary but somewhere in me a dam had burst and I had no means of stopping it. Marty was away more and more and the lead-up to the Christmas was terrible.

I cried at Mass that Christmas morning. I couldn't help it and hoped no one would see the tears run down my face, but really I was past caring. The kids and I drove back to the house as Marty headed to the farm. I told them that I needed to pick something up from a friend so I dropped them off. Continuing out the road I found a quiet lane where I parked the car and cried as if my heart had just broken.

Back at the house I cried into the food as I cooked. When Marty came home in the afternoon we had our dinner and afterwards I told him I wanted a separation. By bedtime I had changed my mind but by the middle of the following week I knew there was no going back. I needed to be alone to heal.

On New Year's Eve a group of us went walking in the mountains. Dave was there and the first moment I got him alone I said, 'I feel like I am pregnant and about to deliver; what I do not know. I need to talk. Will you listen?'

He said, 'Come down to my house tomorrow at one.'

I had now known and watched him for more than a year and a half and I needed to trust someone so I listened to the voice screaming in me, 'Talk to him.'

I had no idea where to start but I was aware that I needed to blame someone and he was as good a one as any and the closest to a British soldier I would ever get – or so I thought.

It was as if there was a child in me wanting to speak, a child who had been silenced for many years. I spoke like a child about the flashbacks that I was having and how I could not get past that gun at my head. It was in freeze-frame and I needed to move on, I cried and cried as I said the first thing that came into my head and when I left a few hours later I felt a ton lighter.

That night Monica's husband, Kevin, was running a dance for the New Year and Marty and I went. It was a cold night. The ground was covered in snow before the frost came and very few appeared so we had a ballroom in the hotel to ourselves. There were only about ten of us and we had a blast.

Kevin played all kinds of music and as I love to dance I never left the floor. I felt so free. That day I had found my voice. I had never told another human being what happened to me and I truly believed it was over and that I was totally free. I danced the dance of pure freedom.

We got home in the early hours of the morning and I passed out peacefully. Three hours later I was in the kitchen wanting to bang my head off the wall. There was so much more there. I could not believe it. I now understood that I had opened a can of worms and they had begun to crawl out. At nine I called Dave and said I needed to come back. 'I have more to say.'

'I know,' he said, 'you have only started.'

Back I went that afternoon and this continued until the bulk of what I had to say was said. I needed to express so many things. I would talk and cry and cry and talk and go home exhausted and wait for the next memory to appear. This happened again and again and again. It was like a pot of water boiling: as soon as the steam disappeared more was produced.

'Is there a possibility I could be making all this up?' I asked Dave one day.

'Do you think you are?'

'No, but I don't understand why I am remembering this only now.'

'Because, Mary, it's only now that you are strong enough.'

I didn't feel that strong, I just wanted it all to go away.

Marty did not like it at all and said to me one day, 'Why do you need to talk to that man?'

'Because I have to tell someone what happened to me.' Thinking he might want to listen I said, 'I don't need to tell *him*. I need to tell someone. I can tell you.' He did not answer and I continued to talk to Dave.

I would go back in time as I was talking to him, He kept asking me, 'What age are you now?' and I kept repeating, 'I am twelve.' I did not seem to be able to get past the age of twelve.

It was much later that I realised that I was twelve in 1972 when 495 people were murdered in the North, when fear was as much part of our lives as breathing. The worst year of the Troubles in terms of deaths: twice as many were killed that year as there were in the second-worst year over the period of the Troubles.

We still went walking nearly every Sunday and I would talk to Dave as we walked. It was time, time to free myself from the burden of my secrets and I trusted that this man would not repeat anything I would say.

My teenage years were full of secrets. If you saw anything unusual you said nothing. You were putting a burden on someone else if you told and I never told. You kept your secrets and everyone else kept theirs. The war was now over and even the secrets needed to be released for peace to find its place in my heart.

Around that time the children had finally convinced me to get them a dog but of course it was I who was left to care for it and take it for walks. One morning Patch and I were walking in the demesne, which has an entrance beside my house, and I froze. I literally froze and the dog dragged me back to the house like a zombie. It was as if something that I could not cope with was on the verge of coming out and I froze to stop it. I walked after Patch, tears running down my face, tears I could not hold back. I was petrified.

We met nobody but I don't think I would have cared. As soon as I closed the hall door behind me I sat on the floor and screamed as I witnessed a scene from my past that I had held in storage.

With all the effort I could muster I dragged myself to the bed and under the blankets and stayed there for over an hour, shaking and screaming, totally out of control. When a break eventually came I tried to do some breathing to calm down but I was very frightened. I called Dave. He was not there so I left a message and he called back later.

'Where are you?' he said.

'In the back of my brother's car,' I replied without hesitation.

'What are you doing there?'

All I could say is, 'They're going to shoot us. They're going to shoot us.'

'They can't harm you, Mary,' he said gently. 'They can't harm you now.

'But they can! They can kill us! They can do whatever they want. They can kill us!'

'No, Mary, they can't,' he said. 'It's all over now. You did not feel the pain when it was going in. You are feeling the pain of it coming out. Stay with it and let it go. What happened?'

'We were coming around McManuses' corner and they stopped us and searched us and as we were getting back into the car they said they would shoot us before we reached the next corner.'

I was still in that car. It was as if I had just frozen it in time and it was back with the fear and pain that I had blocked that day.

'They are kneeling on the road, three soldiers with their guns aimed at the back of the car. We are lying on the floor of the car. There is someone else with me but I don't know who. All I know is that we are going to die. They have the right to shoot us and no one will ever ask why.' I cried uncontrollable tears.

'Stay with it, Mary,' he said, 'and I'll call you back later.'

I screamed and screamed; the child in me who never had the chance that day, the child who lay in silence in the back of the car. Part of my body had never reached the next corner. I wrote this poem years earlier when I did not understand what it meant.

Fear

Silence, deadly silence, I lay there,
Guns pointed at the car,
Fear, paralysing fear.
Thirty year later I still fear.
I cannot move,
I cannot move on.
I fear.
What if the match is lost in the replay?

I was afraid to move as I was still in that car and part of me had no idea what the outcome was. Now there was someone at the other end of a phone so I let go it go in slow motion as the car got to the corner and around it. I lay exhausted in my bed. At three o'clock I got up, washed my face and went to pick my children up at school.

As I fed the children later, the phone rang. A man's voice said, 'Hi, Mary, do you have a bed for me for the night?'

It was Noel, my brother.

'No problem. Do you want dinner?'

It was Noel who was driving the car that day. Noel is a quiet man who would call in to see me when I was up home but he rarely rang and never before had he stayed except when he was working for me.

Well, I thought, I would have to ask him.

After dinner, as we sat alone at the kitchen table, I told him what I remembered, and asked him, 'Do you remember?'

'Not that particular time, Mary, but it happened so often I would not remember them all.'

We had never talked about the Troubles before and I was not going to let this opportunity go. 'Do you remember the searches?' I asked. 'Were they as bad as I remember?'

'No, they were worse.'

'I'm not mad. These things did happen to us.'

I was helping myself and the world was supporting me. I had lost all belief in God but knew I was being guided. I told Marty nothing about this, as there was now no communication between us. I needed time alone to get better and I wanted the kids to know what was happening to me, I wanted the freedom to cry and to deal with this.

I asked Marty to leave. He didn't answer.

Well, I thought, then I am going to have to go to a solicitor. My solicitor had upped and married a girl from Belfast and moved up north so I needed a new one. Somebody gave me the name of a woman and off I went to meet her.

I liked Brid as soon as I saw her and after I told her my story she said, 'We'll write to him.' I was glad I had shared this with someone else, as the only member of my family who knew that there was a problem in my marriage was my sister Geraldine. I had confided in her a long time before and she had listened but made no comment. She knew I would make a decision when the time was right but she never influenced it. She liked Marty but she knew it was not working out.

We had bought the house next door a few years before and it was rented to pay the mortgage. Someone had to move and as my business was in our home I wanted to stay. This house had been rented to a woman and her little daughter for nearly three years. After a lot of thought I knew I had no choice but to ask her to give the house back to us. It was where Marty wanted to be. Everything was coming to a head and it had to be dealt with.

One night, after putting the job off many times, I went over to see her. I hated to ask her to leave but we needed the house. My heart was thumping as I went to the door to explain the situation. I said, 'Stay until you find something suitable and I'll help you.'

'Don't worry about it,' she said. 'I was going to move out in the next month anyway so I'll move sooner to facilitate you.' I couldn't believe it. Everything was falling into place.

I told Marty and we agreed a date he would move. Jarlath was twelve on his Confirmation day and Marty was to leave the following week and take the children on Wednesdays and Sundays. I walked out of the church and my marriage the next week. All the supports I believed I had were gone, yet I knew this was the right thing to do.

I had been going to church all my life and now I knew it was time to move on. I wanted to find myself and I did not need any more rules and regulations to restrict me from doing this. I figured I was adult enough to make my own decisions and had seen too many problems caused by the church.

I think the final straw was when, at a meeting one night, a woman I knew well who was very religious said, 'But we have the one and only true [Catholic] church.' It sent a shiver down my spine. It was what I had heard as a child but then people from another religion said it. I didn't consider myself any better or any worse than anyone else and could no longer believe that, if there was a God, he considered one person better than another. If he did I wanted nothing to do with him.

I took the kids up home and when I got back Marty had moved. It was a very sad day.

When we got back I sat the children down at the kitchen table and said to them, 'I am suffering from post-traumatic stress and if you come into a room and I'm crying it's okay. I will be okay but I have to cry for all the times I didn't in the past when I should have.

There's nothing to worry about. I'll be fine.'

By this time I knew from experience that children need to know what's going on. We were never told things so we would be protected and now I was trying to deal with all the things we were protected from. I know it was hard for them and they used to cry too. They missed their daddy but he was only next door and they could come and go as they pleased.

20

THE WEIGHT OF SECRETS

I was now free for two nights each week, alone to deal with my past. Everything settled down in time, everything, that is, except my memories. They were coming constantly now and I tried to contain them to the nights I was alone and the children were gone or asleep. I had been given the time and my body and mind took advantage of it.

I continued to talk to Dave after class or out walking and the more I told him the more I remembered. It was like a volcano erupting and as the lava flowed it burned into the core of my being.

Now when I went up home I asked more and more questions and I started to read pieces from books about the Troubles. It was a difficult but fascinating experience putting the pieces of the jigsaw back together, like the time when I realised that 1972 was one the worst years or when I read that the IRA were much more active in the winter months when most of the day was in darkness.

This fascinated me because all my life no matter where I lived I would start to wake at five in the morning as soon as the time changed back. My body was preparing for the raids, which were much more frequent in the winter months. Now that I understood it I could deal with it. I would go into my meditation and talk to myself, explain to a frightened child that the war was over and everything was going to be okay.

I remember once phoning a friend and saying, 'Sometimes I wish I could go into the psychiatric unit and be put out for a week.' I was exhausted.

A psychiatrist from Belfast called me, a lady who was working with ex-prisoners and their families. A friend had asked her to call me, someone who was worried about me, someone who cared.

'How are you?' she asked.

'I don't know,' I replied. 'Sometimes I have memories of things I can't believe happened to me and I know I'm not mad. They are very real and it scares me at times.'

'Who are you talking to?

I told her.

'Do you trust him?'

'Yes.'

'Then tell him everything,' she said. 'Tell the same person everything.'

'I start to shake and I get these flashes of things in my head and I just cry and cry and cry.'

'You are having flashbacks.'

'Am I the only one?'

'No.'

I didn't ask where the others were. At least, I thought, I am not alone.

My sister Geraldine and I decided to go on holiday to Lanzarote, to get me away from it all. I did not tell my family what I was going through but they knew I was having a tough time.

It has to end some time, I thought, but I could see no end in sight. I was coping but just about. I was off all medication, both natural and chemical, and I could eat, which was a huge improvement.

Off I went on the train to Dublin to meet Geraldine. I felt so lost. I remember thinking I would gladly get off in Roscommon and go to the psychiatric unit. I knew I was going to be lost without my children but that they would be fine.

Dad and Mam came to stay in my house and off I went. Even though we got on well, Geraldine and I had not spent more than a night in the same place for more than twenty years. She is very sharp and I was very fragile and vulnerable. We spent the night in Peter's house in Dublin and flew out the next day.

I had been in Lanzarote before. It was hot when we arrived and I always found comfort in heat – and I needed comfort. On the first day we decided we would be doing neither cleaning nor cooking so we spent most of the week stepping over clothes on the floor as we went out to eat. We spent the days in our hired car driving around the island.

We shared a room, which made me nervous, as I didn't want Geraldine to hear me crying at night. Sometimes I would just lie there and weep; sometimes I'd go into the bathroom and sit on the floor and cry into a towel. I was so used to being able to do this in the privacy of my own bedroom that I felt restricted.

Geraldine was very good to me and I told her all that was happening as we drove around in the sun. She asked me what I remembered and I told her about the last flashback when I had this vision of me standing at the bottom of the stairs at home. Seán was trying to run up and Mammy was holding him by his leg, pleading with him not to jump out the back window – that they would shoot him. I stood there and could do nothing.

'I know,' she said. 'I remember it too. I was standing next to you.'

I enjoyed the week but was glad to get home to the children and the comfort of being in my own space.

At times I would be so angry I would go out into the bog to be alone so that I could release some anger with a stick. I would beat down the nettles until I had pains in my arms and shoulder from the force I used. By this time I had broken all Jarlath's golf clubs and his hurley. I remember once getting up in the middle of the night and sitting under the counter-top in the kitchen, shaking and angry. I thought if I broke every window of the house it would only take the steam off the anger. Feeling so helpless and with no one to turn to I asked, 'If there is anything out there, please help me.'

I started shaking uncontrollably. It was like a convulsion as I completely let go. My whole body shook and ten minutes later I was back in bed and fell asleep like a baby.

I had time alone and all hell had broken loose in my body. No one knew what was happening to me, even myself.

If something was forcing its way out when I was not in an appropriate place to deal with it I would try to hold it until I got to the sanctuary of my bedroom, away from the children.

Flashbacks

My hands shake, my body shakes, I make a fist.
Can I hold on to it, can I hold it in my fist?
I am not free to let it go,
But how long can I hold on?
I drive through the small town, home to my refuge,
The tears running from beneath my glasses,
I wave at people I know,

> *They don't know what's happening to me,*
> *But then neither do I.*

How could I tell anyone any about this, especially members of my family who seemed to be coping so well?

Jarlath would sometimes find me crying. He would always say 'Can I get you anything, Mammy?'

'No, pet. It's okay. I'll be okay.'

But he would get me a glass of water and leave it beside me with the phone and say, 'I'm going to play with my friends. Call me if you need me.' It always made me smile. I felt so guilty when he or Roisín found me like this but there were just some times when it could not be controlled.

I did not want to be dependent on anyone. I wanted to be able to find my own answers but right then I was like a newborn foal, trying my best to stand on my own two feet.

It was a very difficult time as I had always been so independent. I had always been able to fend for myself but all this was on the surface. I was always physically and financially independent, but emotionally I was a child, a child who had never had the chance to grow, who was emotionally stunted by a war.

This was my emotional growth, which should have happened when I was a teenager. It was very difficult as I was now in my mid-forties. It is normal to spend a long period of time growing naturally. I had to grow in a few hours on a dark winter's night and it was guns, not time, that triggered my growth. I was like the tomato that is ripened too fast: it looks perfectly normal but it's never the same as the one ripened in the natural sunlight.

Mine was not a normal growth: it was forced and now I was trying to mature. As the hard exterior was caving in, the soft interior was trying to survive in a world it had never experienced.

I had hidden behind Marty for nearly twenty years and now I had no one to shield me and I was forced to face a lot of things that I could have chosen to leave alone. But the idea of dependence was not something I relished the thought of, not after my episode with prescription drugs. No one seemed to know what I was going through and it was years later that I finally met anyone who had suffered like me. But I was determined to face whatever it was: the alternative was no longer an option.

I was on a mission and the mission was to get myself better.

I had opened Pandora's box and had no idea what would come next but I knew my healing would have to come from within if I wanted the independence that I craved.

For now I had to trust someone to listen to me and even though I did not need to talk as much as before I continued to tell Dave the secrets I had hidden for far too long. It was a relief to share them as I no longer had the strength to carry the weight of them alone.

21

RELEASING MY PRISONERS

The soldier at the side of my bed with the gun to my head seemed to be my constant companion and I could not remember anything past that freeze-frame. I had to let him go to move on but I was frightened of what came next. Like the poem I wrote at one time, part of me was afraid that if I started to look at it I'd find that he did shoot me and I died. Part of me was certainly dead and I needed to go back there to bring it back to life and bring my present life back to some semblance of normality.

Before I started Tai Chi I spent nearly twenty years doing yoga every day, a routine I had designed for myself to stay flexible. Yoga and meditation, which I practised twice a day, had sustained me. I stopped practising yoga and now Tai Chi was making me stronger but it was time to go further and I followed my gut as to where to go next.

My stomach was getting upset again so I decided to check out food allergies to see what my body was having a problem digesting. Well aware that it was much more than food, I was looking for a short-term solution to keep it at bay, as I didn't think I could cope with much more.

The therapist also practised kinesiology and while I was in her office she asked if I would be willing to try it. She felt that my stomach problems came from something deeper than food allergies. In the process of doing her tests she said, 'You have a problem with your father.'

'No,' I replied. 'I love my father. He's great.'

'You have a blockage there,' she continued.

She explained that she could give me herbs to release whatever it was and other herbs to help me cope with whatever came up, I said fine as I was quite sure she had no idea what she was talking about. I had been taking the herbs only a few days when they started to move things. I was taking Jarlath and his friends to Foxford for the night. Up to that I had no memory of anything but the gun at my head and the soldier at the side of my bed. Well, that was all about to change!

The kids wanted to go up into the mountains for a walk when we arrived at the cottage so I got them all out in the best gear they had and led them up to the top of the first peak. They brought a picnic and wanted to stop to eat and mess around by themselves. I left them and continued alone, telling them to call me when they wanted either to move on or go back.

Walking on alone, away from the noise of four teenagers I was surprised when my heart started to pound and I began to shake. It was as if someone had restarted the movie that had been stuck in my mind for over thirty years. I found shelter behind a rock and stayed there with my back up against it. I knew there was no way I could stop this and I would have to deal with it as best I could. I knew I was being protected by something and all I could do was trust.

I could see myself getting out of a bed. In fact I was back in that room with all the fear I had blocked at the time. I lay behind the rock and twisted in pain as the memories pushed through; three soldiers took the four young girls from their beds at gunpoint and kept us there. I shall never forget the sounds that came from me that day. They were like those of a wounded animal.

The movie in my mind continued, moving from the bedroom out into the corridor, where the rest of the children were being forced along at gunpoint, down the stairs.

As I walked down the stairs I was thinking, 'It will be okay when we get to the kitchen. Daddy will be there. Daddy will sort it out.' But when I got there and looked at Daddy, I saw that he was in bits. I could not understand how he could do nothing. He was our protector. There was a war outside our door but this was our home and Daddy was in control here. But not any more. We were all forced into the kitchen and into a corner by men in uniform, carrying guns. They screamed and shouted at us. Ten children and not a sound. Not one of us spoke. Not one of us cried but the baby, who was inconsolable. Not one of us could move to comfort her.

My Mother

She stood in her own kitchen,
He stood in front of her in a foreign land.
She had ten children behind her,
He had an army and two governments.
Where is your son? he said?
I don't know, she replied.
You don't know where your fucking son is, he spat
No, she answered. Does your mother know where you are?

That night I realised that your parents could not protect you from everything and that day in the mountains was the first time I could go back to the memory of the gun at my head and trust that I really did survive. It was as if part of my life was still in that bedroom, part of my fear was still in that bedroom and part of my healing was still in that same bedroom.

I still told Dave everything that was happening to me as I did not want to go over the edge. If I did, I wanted someone to know what edge I had gone over so that they could help me to get back. I could not reach him that weekend so I continued this process myself as best I could as there was no way of stopping it.

When the process in the mountains finished I could barely talk. I called Jarlath and he told me that he and his friends had made their way back to the house. With the noise and excitement he noticed nothing. I came down the mountain slowly, afraid of what was to come next.

It took all my strength to drive home but I did and later, with the children in bed, I took a hot water bottle, which was my only companion in bed now, sat up and knew instinctively that I needed to go back into that room in my meditation and face the soldier.

Now I was not only meditating but using visualisation. I could bring myself back to any time or place and visualise myself there, and if I needed to be comforted, I would comfort that part of me.

When things were really bad I would take myself at whatever age I had been at that time into a wee room I had created in me, a room no one could enter but me, a room that was full of love, light and peace. In my meditation I would visit the room to check the progress of the child in this healing place.

The Recovery Room

I have a room, a room deep within my being,
Accessed only through my mind,
A room for healing,
I have taken you there, one by one,
Time after time,
From all kinds of situations
I bathe you there and put you into a bed,
Where no one can get to you but me,
I am the only visitor; you are secure and safe,
Safe to lie there,
Until there is enough trust in me,
That you rise and talk or scream,
Or whatever is necessary.
I visit you there whenever I have a free moment,
And hug you,
And love you,
And allow you to take your time to heal,
And sometimes when I'm lost and lonely in this world,
I go there too for comfort and love.

Later Andy, my psychotherapist, asked me who taught me to do this and I told him I had created this place myself as I had nowhere else to go and no one else to turn to. I realised you can heal yourself when you let everything and everyone else go.

I visualised the soldier in the room with me, alone and unarmed. I followed my own guidance on this; I knew intuitively what to do so, facing him unarmed, I told him what I thought of him and it was not nice. I told him that his actions had affected my whole life and that now in my forties I was trying to put the pieces together again for my own sanity, to try to live a normal life.

I said everything I needed to say and he listened. He had no choice as I had tied him up and gagged him. Before I finished with him that night, I kicked him and beat him with a hurley. Exhausted, I fell asleep.

Over the next few days I held him there, captive in my mind, and visited him in my meditations. He had been there for more than thirty years so I was in no hurry to let him go. He certainly wasn't going anywhere until I was finished with him.

Three days later I released him and before he left the room and my life, I hugged him and said, 'I hope you survived the Troubles and are happy.' As I released him I realised I had released myself and found another way to heal.

The Soldier

You burst into my room at 5am as I lay in the dreams of a child,
You were prepared and equipped,
I was innocent and vulnerable.
You stood at my bedside and woke me with the point of your
*   gun,*
I awoke petrified,
You had no mercy,
I had no protection.
You left my home hours later, but not my mind nor my
*   nightmares.*
Thirty-five years later I release you,
To release me,
Go in peace,
I do not fear you any longer.

Now I knew that if I could do this with one person I could do it with others, whether they were from my past or in the present. I also realised I could do it with myself and the parts of me that were stuck in the past.

One night not long afterwards I had a dream that I was in a hotel lobby. I walked over to the elevator to go up to my bedroom. I stepped in and was alone. As the elevator moved it went down instead of up and it stopped in the basement. The door opened and I was facing a dark space. I woke up.

I knew it was one of those significant dreams that meant something but I had no idea what – so the next time I was going into a meditation I decided to start it where my dream had ended.

After I did my breathing exercises I brought myself back into the elevator, facing that dark open space, and I knew there was someone out there. My wee voice said, 'You have two choices. You can press a button and go up or you can go out into the space and see what is there.' I hesitated, but only for a moment. I knew I might never get this opportunity again.

I stepped out of the elevator and it closed behind me. I was left alone in darkness in a place I could describe only as being like a subway station in New York City. There was a pillar in front of me and I knew that behind it was something I had a choice to look at or not. I ventured on in the dark and behind the pillar sat a girl, a young girl who looked like she was starved and without any feeling.

Immediately I knew that the girl was me or a part of me that had been left in the dark for far too long and I could choose either to leave her there or pick her up and take her out into the open.

I did not hesitate. I picked up the bag of bones that she was and carried her up the stairway into the light of day. From there I took her into my wee room and made up a bed in the corner where I lay with her and told her I was so sorry for taking so long to find her. I wept and she lay motionless.

Over the following days I went to visit her a few times a day in meditations – whether for a few minutes or for a half a hour – and a few days later when I got there she was gone.

'Where are you?' I asked. In a split second I was in a big open field with the sun beaming down on me. She lay half-sheltered under a big oak tree.

She smiled for the first time and it was then I knew that she was going to be okay. I also knew that I had found my real self, the self that I had hidden in the darkness as I conformed to the norms of society in order to be accepted.

22

Acknowledging
My Own Healing Powers

Now that I knew how to deal with this myself. I did not want to be dependent on another person for support all the time. I stopped going to Tai Chi class and walking in order to ground myself in this new way of working on myself.

A few months later I was back in class, much stronger and with more confidence in my own healing powers. I was beginning to trust myself more and more and listen very carefully to my inner voice. It was then that I realised that the power was in me, not anyone else. Now I was attracting into my life the people and things I needed to help me in any way I needed help.

My marriage was truly over, I doubted if Marty would recognise who I had become. He had settled in next door. We had property to divide and all was sorted except for a building we had in the town. I felt it should be mine but Marty wanted half of it so we had stalemate for over a year. It was getting me down so when I woke one morning and a little voice said, 'Give him half,' I did not hesitate and called him immediately.

We were going to have to sell it and divide the proceeds and that was okay. I had decided it would help pay off some of my huge loans.

One day as I was walking in the mountains, I discussed this with a friend and told her the building was going on the market that week. As I drove home that evening my wee business voice said, 'Buy Marty out of his share.'

I listened very carefully as always. I trusted this little voice. Even though this building was vacant and in a mess with no income from it, I ruled nothing out.

I decided to do a meditation and see what came up so later that evening I went to my own little private world. I had come to love this world over the years but now I loved it even more because I was using it to help in everyday situations. I visualised myself in the room I had created for myself. I asked myself if I should buy him out.

I visualised myself on chairs at both sides of a big open fire: one part of me would talk to the other. My body and soul is what I believe they are. The 'body' is the emotional side and the 'soul' is this very calm part of me that seems to have all the answers but none of the emotions.

'Should we buy?' my body asked.

'Yes!' answered my soul.

So the decision was made even though it was a big one as I already owed a lot of money and now had to borrow more, but I had never questioned this before and was not about to now.

Over to Marty I went. I sat down with him and said, 'I'll buy you out of the building.'

'You're mad!' he said.

Maybe he was right and he was not the only person to say it to me but I trusted myself. My inner voice was telling me to buy, so I was going to buy.

'Maybe I'm mad,' I replied, 'but think about how much you want for it and I'll be back over tomorrow and we can sort it.'

I really had no idea what I was doing. Renting had become impossible with all the new houses in town and the shop had only rented twice for two short periods of time in the previous five years but my gut was telling me to buy and I was not going to argue.

With all this in mind I called back over to see Marty the next day. We haggled a bit and I agreed to pay him more than I had wanted to pay but my gut said, 'Buy him out,' and the deal was done. Now I had to approach the bank to look for the money. Banks never really bothered me because I knew if I wanted something I could convince them to give me a loan. I had a good track record but I had no idea how I was going to present this to them. But I knew if I was to buy I would be shown a way to meet the repayments.

In the kitchen later that evening as I prepared the dinner for the kids and teas for the patients. I told Jarlath what I was planning to do. I told Jarlath everything I did in business and why I did it because he was interested.

Roisín's head was in music and media and she needed a lot of points in her Leaving Cert to get into the third level course she wanted. If I talked to her about business she would listen but not take in a word of it.

Jarlath asked a lot of questions that evening. When I could not answer I would say, 'Sometimes, Ja, you just know what to do and you have to follow that knowing.'

In the middle of the dinner the phone rang and a woman asked to speak to me. 'You own that building beside the school in town.'

'Yes,' I replied absentmindedly.

'Would you rent the shop?'

I nearly dropped the phone. 'Yes, of course. What do you want it for?'

'A launderette,' she answered and we agreed to meet a little later for her to see it.

Jarlath was amazed and I was too but really I could write a book about how often this had happened to me. I was now very aware of it and watched with interest – as did Jarlath.

Off I went down that night to meet her. We had agreed a price for the rent before I left her with the key so that she could bring her family to see it later. When I got to the bank the next day the shop was rented and I had the means to pay off the loan that I needed to buy Marty out.

I've always said: in life you need a good doctor, a good solicitor, a good bank manager, a good accountant and good friends. I had them all but now I would say that all you really need is good trust in yourself. To find this, all you need to do is take the time to visit yourself. Spend time alone with yourself.

The loan was sanctioned, Marty was paid, the laundry was opened and the mortgage was met.

'This,' I told Rosin and Jarlath, 'is the only way to live – by trust.'

Six months later the people renting the shop wanted to move. I was shocked as I did not expect this. I had huge repayments but I knew I would have to go back into the meditation and my little room. Before I had finished the meditation I knew it was time to sell.

Selling was not a thing I had done that much of – accumulating was what I did best – but I was changing, so I picked up the phone and called a local auctioneer whom I considered a good businessman.

'Seamus, would my building in town sell?'

'Are you ready to sell?'

'Yes.'

'Is all in order and are the deeds in your name?'

'Yes.'

The legal separation was completed now and all the properties and mortgages were in the rightful names.

'Come to see me in the morning with confirmation of this. I think I have a buyer for you.'

Now most people would say, 'Isn't that what they always say?' but I knew different. I knew it was a sign that it was the right time.

I called my solicitor and she faxed the information through to the auctioneer's office and he had it in his hand when I arrived next morning.

'How much do want for it?'

'What is it worth?

He named a price that I was very happy with; I knew what my building was worth and it was a lot more than the year before.

'Okay, see what you can do.'

'I may be able to get more but we'll start at that.'

I left it in his capable hands.

The next day was Saturday and Dave and I were doing a weekend of Tai Chi, meditation and hill-walking at my house in Foxford. I had ideas of moving down there when the kids were finished school and wanted to see if there was any interest in the facility I was offering.

When I came down from the mountains, there was a message on my answering machine from Seamus.

'I have an offer for you,' he said, when I phoned him, and he named the price he had put on the building.

'Take it!'

'We may get a bit more. There might be others interested.'

'Do the people interested have the money to buy?'

'Yes.'

'Then take it.'

'Let me check out a few other people who have an interest in it.'

'Okay, but close the deal by Monday at five. I've got what I wanted and I want it sold.' Could I believe it? Yes I could, but I was delighted.

The sale was closed on Monday at five and the deal went through as quickly as it possibly could with no hitches.

I had followed my gut and taken a chance. Six months after I bought Marty out, I sold the property and had enough money to pay off most of my loans. I trusted the world and I was rewarded. I had got a fair price for a building and the buyer was happy too. When something is right, everyone should walk away happy, knowing it's time to move on.

23

Taking Responsibility for Myself

I now had more time to read, walk and work on healing myself and teaching the children what life was really about. It's not about what you own or what you have achieved. Life is about you, who you are, what you are here for. Life is about learning that until you give yourself what you need you cannot expect it of anybody else and that everything comes from yourself. You get what you give and life is much more than what meets the eye.

The separation was now final and Marty and I were free to move on. Roisín was working hard in school to achieve her goal to get into Media Studies. As a child she spent her time with her friends making movies and plays and now she had decided that this is what she wanted to do for her life.

Jarlath was doing as little as possible. He had run wild after the separation and my heart was broken by calls from the school about him. He was not only doing nothing himself but keeping everyone else back with his antics in the classroom. It was a full-time job trying to keep him in line.

After the break I took alone in Lanzarote, I came back with strength to sort out a lot of things and Jarlath was one of them. Just before he was to start school again in September to do his Junior Cert and Roisín her Leaving, I decided it was time to set him straight on a few things.

We were coming from Galway one day, just the two of in the car – a place that I found great to talk to the children as they had no choice but to listen. 'Jarlath,' I said, 'when you go back to school next week to prepare for your exams next year I do not care if you do anything or even if you fail your exams. You know I have always told you that you do your schoolwork for yourself, not for me. I will love you no matter what you decide to do, but if you continue to disrupt class I will take you out of the school and send you to a boarding school. You have a right to do nothing but you have no right to stop others learning.'

He laughed, 'You don't mean that, Mammy!'

'Yes I do, Jarlath. Try me. Roisín is doing her Leaving Cert and will get all the help she needs from me to make this year as easy as possible for her so she can concentrate on her studies. You can do as you wish. It is your choice. Take responsibility for yourself. You are free to make your own choices. I am your guide, not your controller.' He was fourteen.

Roisín was always stuck in her books with her headphones on listening to music but she was getting the results she needed.

Jarlath would now try to show me at night what he was doing. 'It's okay,' I said. 'If you are doing your work, good for you, but there is no need for me to see it.'

I know I sounded hard but this boy had driven me to the edge. At least I was getting no more calls from the school, which was good enough for me. I was learning to practise tough love.

A few months later we had our parent-teacher meeting, something that had been a pleasure in my life until Jarlath started secondary school, when it had become a nightmare! I went down, nervous as usual, knowing I would get glowing reports about Roisín and God know what about Jarlath. But I was in for a surprise. There was a smile on most of the teachers' faces when they mentioned Jarlath. Not only did they tell me that he had much more manners but that he had started to do a little work – not much but a little. I was delighted and had no problems telling him this.

'Jarlath,' I said, 'manners will take you a lot further than an education but if you have both you can go anywhere. You are a lovely young man.' It was the truth: he would charm the birds off the trees.

As the exams approached Jarlath seemed to be doing no studying at all but one night he shouted out of his bedroom, 'I'm studying, Mam. Can I have a cup of tea?'

I was at this point making it as easy for Roisín as I possibly could, getting and giving her what she needed so that she had all the facilities to study.

Jarlath I ignored, as he seemed to have no interest. When I brought in the tea that night he had his head in a book, which was probably upside down but I never even looked. He has to take responsibility for himself, I thought, as I headed out of the room.

'I am studying,' he reiterated as I went out the door.

'Look Jarlath, if you fail everything I will love just as much as I do now. If you do anything, do it for yourself, not for me.' I walked back and give him a hug.

The exams started with Roisín in a panic. She had her sights on Media in Maynooth, which was her single-minded goal, and she would not put a second choice on her CEO form.

'If I don't get Media, I'll go back to school and do my Leaving again.'

Well, I thought, at least she knows what she wants.

They were both doing art and I remember the day of that exam so well, Roisín had tried every medium – watercolours, oils, and charcoals – then finally decided on pencils, after I had worn a path to the art shop in Roscommon. I had no idea what Jarlath was doing. I never asked and I had not even realised he was doing his Art exam the same day as her. She was fussing about the house that morning and I was glad when it was time to bring her down to the school. As we were leaving the house to go to the car I asked Jarlath, 'Do you have Art today too?'

'Ya. Would you have a pencil?'

I burst out laughing and I got him one

Getting closer to the school he said. 'You wouldn't have a rubber, Mam?'

'No! I forgot my pencil case.'

At the gates of the school I produced my bottle of Rescue Remedy. I put drops in the bottles of water of both Roisín and her friend to keep them calm as they did their exams.

'Do you want some?' I asked Jarlath.

'What would I need that for?' he said as he got out of the car, cool as a cucumber.

'What indeed!' I thought.

With all the exams over, Roisín was counting up the marks she thought she would get. The night before the results came out she was counting again and she drove Jarlath and me mad. I reminded her what I had said to her all through her exams and for the previous few years. Just concentrate on what you need; you don't have to know how you are going to get it. Leave that to a power bigger than you and it will work out perfectly – it always has.'

The day finally arrived and I dropped her at the school, a bag of nerves. She believed that her future depended on these results. She called me later to tell me she got five points more than she needed.

'Brilliant!' I said, as I listened to her excited voice. 'I knew you would.'

'I did not get as much in Art as I thought I should and I got more in Home Economics than I expected.'

'Roisín, you've got what you wanted. Let the rest go and enjoy it. It does not matter how it adds up as long as it adds up.'

That was the first hurdle over. Next came the offers and she was accepted into the course she wanted.

'Guess what, Mammy?' she said later, as she checked her letter of offer, 'the points went up five this year and I had just enough.'

We both smiled. She's learning, I thought.

Roisín deferred her university place for a year and did a media course as she needed a break from too much studying and was only seventeen. I remember the day I left her and her three friends to Galway; they were going to share a flat in the city centre for the next year. I was sad; she was moving on. She was a pleasure to live with but, as someone had once said to me, you have to give your children roots and wings. I hoped I had given her roots and it was now time to give her wings.

At seventeen Roisín was the oldest of her flatmates. She was happy to leave the small town behind her as she started on her journey to the rest of her life.

The following month Jarlath's exam results came through. He did okay but not as well as any of his friends and I said, 'Look what you got when you did nothing! Can you imagine what you could have got if you studied?' He never answered.

Jarlath was a brilliant footballer, which was occupying a lot of his time. He took after his father. When the local team won the Under-16 County Championship he was the captain and Marty was the manager. My friend Anne and I stood on the sidelines and screamed as we had at every match since our children started playing together at eight. It meant more to them and us than winning the World Cup.

Back at school, he starting his Leaving Cert course and did what he had to do and little more. About a year later something clicked and he started to work. When he did his exams he did far better than he or I expected and he surprised us both when he decided he wanted to go to college. He had decided that he loved studying.

By this time Roisín had finished up in Galway with great results and cried as she moved on to Maynooth to do her degree. A few weeks later she forgot about Galway as she made new friends in County Kildare. I had taught her that if you trust you will get exactly what you want – if it is right for you. Media was right for her.

24

EVERYTHING HAPPENS
AT EXACTLY THE RIGHT TIME

Throughout those years, when the kids were going through school, I was still having flashbacks and nightmares. I had tried many places to get help but to no avail. Nobody seemed to understand what I was talking about or what I was going through, even my family.

I tried to get back to the psychiatrist in Belfast but was not able to get her number, so I coped as best I could in the situation I was in.

So many things would trigger off memories. I avoided any-thing on television concerning the Troubles and I rarely watched the news. In time I found it easier to speak to people about it, especially when we were walking in the mountains. There I would bring it up if I got a chance. I had no problem telling people about my background and if it changed how they felt about me, it didn't bother me any longer.

In the car when I was alone listening to the radio, a few words or even a song could send my whole body into a spin. All I could do was grip the steering wheel as tight as possible and scream. I would scream until I was exhausted and then it would take days for me to recover. This happened often but I had no other way to deal with it. It was a short-term solution but it was the only way I knew.

Once I was on a walk that I had been doing for years. As I approached the railway line there were five men in front of me. They were probably working on the line but nothing would convince me that they were not police or soldiers. It was totally illogical for me to be petrified but petrified is exactly how I felt. I tried to force one foot in front of another to walk on but my body had completely frozen and my heart was thumping so loudly I thought the neighbours would hear it. It was crazy, maybe *I* was crazy, but all I could do was turn back and make my way home to bed, where I lay under the blankets and sobbed my heart out.

I tried my best to manage a sometimes unmanageable life and told people what was happening to me, hoping that someone would know someone who could help me.

Around this time, when my kids were both on the verge of leaving the nest, I was considering what I was going to do with the rest of my life. I had my house in Foxford in a place I loved and had ideas of going down there to live and starting another business. The business I had was declining, which suited me, even though I loved it. It was time to move on. It had served its purpose, for me and for the people I was keeping. They were now all much older and in need of the kind of care I was not equipped or qualified to give them. I would be alone and free to live wherever I wished.

Beside the cottage I had renovated in Foxford, my friend Mary had put a site up for sale and everyone used to say to me as we walked by, 'You should buy that, Mary.'

'What do I need a site for, or indeed another project?' I would answer. I was trying to keep my body and soul together. Secretly I was now afraid of extending myself in case I fell flat on my face again, so I would ignore them as I walked on past the beautiful site facing the mountains, with the most beautiful little granary on it, a granary that looked like the gate lodge to the mountains.

Then one day as I was walking past it alone, my wee voice said, 'You should buy the site.'

I was shocked and walked on, but as I continued into the mountains I found myself turning my head again and again as I climbed to the first peak. I kept turning to see what the rest of my body felt about it. Each time I turned I liked the idea more and more but there was that nagging doubt: would it push me over the edge?

The further I walked the clearer the voice was and the further away I got from the little granary the more I wanted to go back and have a good look. Eventually I stopped and searched my rucksack for my binoculars to have a better look without any one noticing me. I lay back in the heather and looked at the clear blue sky and asked, 'For what?'

The answer I got back was, 'You never needed to know before: why do you need to know now?'

'True,' I replied, 'but before I needed the work to keep me from looking at myself.'

The answer was, 'Just do it.'

I went back with my head full of thoughts, stepped in and walked the site. It felt so right. When I walked across the road to Mary to talk to her about it I had already made up my mind, but I said, 'Give me a few days, Mary. I might be interested in your site.'

She was delighted and I went home thinking, 'What do I need it for? Mammy will kill me if I say I'm buying again so I'd better convince myself it's the right thing to do before I mention it to her because she will have a million questions.'

Next morning after my meditation I drove back to Mary and we agreed on a price. I knew it was right.

It took a while to get it all sorted but I was in no hurry. I knew all would become apparent when the time was right. When the deeds eventually came through the only thing I did was reapply for planning because on the original plans the granary was to be knocked. To me, that would have been a sin. This little building was part of the community, part of the mountain, built by local people more than a hundred years before. Maybe this is all I need to do, I thought: make sure the granary is left standing.

When the county council agreed with me I was delighted and filed the planning permission away as I had enough to occupy my mind.

About a year later I woke one day and my wee voice was chattering again. My soul and I were great friends by now, even if I did not like everything it said to me!

'Check your planning permission,' it said.

'I have another four years.'

The next morning I had the same message: 'Check your planning permission.' Again I ignored it, as I was sure I had four more years to build.

The third morning when the voice came through I jumped out of bed, went straight to the filing cabinet and checked. Everything looked fine. It said five years before planning needed to be renewed, but my little voice told me to turn the page.

I found that one of the stipulations was that the house was to be built to roof level before the five years were up. Then it said that this meant five years from the date it was first approved, which, with a little calculation, meant I had seven months to get the house to the roof or look for an extension on the planning permission.

Not one to panic – by now I had found that there really was not much use in it – I called Mark, the architect who had just built a house beside me and asked him what were the chances of getting my planning permission renewed.

'Very low. They have got very strict. You could take a chance, but I wouldn't.'

Well, I thought, that's that, as my mother would say.

My next call was to the county council to explain that I did not realise that planning permission dated from the time of the original approval. They were very polite and told me that they understood the situation but that it was my problem. They would give me an extra year if I got the building to roof level.

What could I say but, 'Thank you.'?

I was in a spin as to what to do next. I knew that selling was out of the question because it would leave the buyers in the same situation as I was in with even less time to sort it. I was left with no choice but to build.

This was going to be a big challenge. It was now coming up to Christmas and everything would be closed down for a few weeks. I had no experience of building from scratch but one thing I had in mind was that I would do it as naturally as possible. I had renovated the little granary the year before using all natural products and a natural energy-efficient house seemed like the way to go.

Later that day Roisín called from Dublin. 'Mammy,' she said, 'I never know what to buy you for Christmas. I'm in Dublin now. What would you like?'

I did not hesitate: 'Get me a book on building an energy-efficient house, if possible written by an Irish author or even an English one. I want it to be suitable for our climate.'

'Okay. What else do you want?'

'Nothing else, Roisín. I need this and nothing else.'

She got the book and I spent the whole of Christmas poring over it and searching the Internet, getting to grips with different materials for building.

My brother Brendan had just returned from the States with his wife Jenny and his daughters, Maria and Elle. Their son James was almost due and Brendie was finishing off the house he had built himself. I called him and he said he would work with me. I knew my other brothers would help when the time came.

I had no experience of the Internet before this but by the time the holidays were over I was expert at finding things. I was on a high again but it was a high that I found easy to walk away from. I accepted all the help the world sent me, which was a lot. I knew I was being guided, that I was on the right path, doing the right thing.

In early January I was back at the bank looking for more money and everything was approved with no problem. The country was booming, so the following spring when Jarlath was preparing for his exams – working well and with no hassle – I was putting down the foundation for our new home and overseeing everything myself.

25

BUILDING FROM SCRATCH

When I started the new house I had a little knowledge both about the site and about using natural products because, the previous summer, I had renovated the wee granary. I added a new roof, wooden windows and doors and an old staircase. Inside I insulated it with hemp and lime to give it a natural finish. I borrowed a small Kango hammer and took off all the old plaster outside. Jarlath and I then pointed it with a lime mortar.

The granary had got its dignity back. I had fought to keep it. It was in the local guide book for the Foxford Way and people would expect it to be there. It looked great with its little red windows and door, back in its natural skin of local stone

I had a big problem with the plans for the new house. It was practical, it was what the county council approved, but, as I had argued with the engineer at the time, it did not blend into the landscape. I wanted something that would look better than a bungalow but because I was fighting to keep the granary at that time I gave in, hoping that when the time came to build, we would work something out with the Council.

The loan was now in order and the bank insisted that an engineer or architect oversee the house and sign it off for payments.

'What would you charge?' I asked Mark Stephens, my architect next-door neighbour to be, knowing he would be more expensive than an engineer.

He said, 'I would give you a good price. I want to do this.' It was as important to him as it was to me that the building should be right. He had built his house next door to my site partly underground and in keeping with the landscape.

I called him later and said, 'Okay, Mark, we'll work together on this.' I emailed him the plans right away and we arranged to meet the next Monday. I was at the kitchen table in the stone cottage on Monday morning when he came in and said, 'How do you like change, Mary?'

'Love it,' I said, as I saw a drawing in his hand, 'but we have no time to change the plans. If we were lucky enough to get it through in three months – and nobody's that lucky these days – we still would not have time.'

By this time I had resigned myself to the bungalow and had planned to make the outside as tasteful as I possibly could.

'Look at this,' he said.

I looked at his drawing and said, 'You've been reading my mind, Mark. This is exactly what I have always had in mind and it is beautiful.'

He had changed the bungalow that I hated into a house a storey-and-a-half high with two roofs. 'If we have two roofs, we can drop the height and the mountains will no longer be blocked as much and it will be much more suitable.' It was his way of saying, 'It won't be so ugly!'

'You'll lose a little space but…'

'I don't care!' I interrupted him. 'It's exactly right. It's like an old schoolhouse with an extension, It will look as if it's always been there. But we still don't have the time.'

'Build it, Mary,' he said. 'Let me worry about the county council. It is right.'

So Brendie and I started the foundations as Mark redrew the plans. I was in heaven: this was right up my street and organisation was one of my strong points.

Brendie was just finishing up his own house, which was beautiful. He is a perfectionist and I knew he would do just as good a job on my house as he did on his own.

Noel had been roofing for over thirty years and is a brilliant carpenter. They gave me the information I needed to get started. By now I had planned to build an ICF (Insulated Concrete Formwork) house and none of them knew anything about it but I had done my homework.

Before Christmas, when I phoned a few suppliers about different things, I asked them all the same question: 'What kind of house would you build for yourself if you were to build today?'

I got all kinds of answers; Block, (hard to make airtight), Wood (too noisy. I wanted a big house and possibly a guesthouse). Then one man said, 'I'd build an ICF house.'

ICF is built with insulation and pumped with concrete, the reverse of a block building, which is built with concrete block and insulated between the blocks. I read about it in my Christmas present, the book from Roisín. I was drawn to it and Googled it. A few days after Christmas, I called a lady who told me all about it. I was sold.

I found a company in Cavan that was starting to produce it. They had been importing and building with it for years. I wanted it to be made in the country if possible as there were would be no shipping involved and my carbon footprint would be smaller.

It would work out a little more expensive but I would have an airtight, mechanically ventilated, energy-efficient house that would need very little heat. I was not going to be questioned on my decisions – not that anyone would have been brave enough to try. It felt right and I knew what I was doing. Anyway, I had my little voice guiding me and I knew everything would be fine.

The foundations were poured in April, on one of the hottest days I have ever experienced. The concrete dried faster than it could be pumped. The man pumping said, 'You're a cool lady,' because I didn't flinch when the lorries were late.

'It will be fine,' I said and it was. We started at seven in the morning and finished at eight that night with Tom, another brother, on site with us.

A week before the insulated blocks were to be delivered I was sitting in a car park in Galway waiting for Jarlath when I got a call from the owner of the company to say that a part had broken in the machinery and they would not be able to deliver for two months.

'I'll give you a good price then if you wait.'

'I can't wait, Tommy. I don't have two months. Who would you recommend?'

He gave me a number in Cork and I called it.

'Jarlath speaking,' was how the phone was answered (a good sign I thought) I had known only three Jarlaths in my whole life and liked them all. Before the conversation was finished I liked another one. The materials we needed were going to be delivered to the site within the week, with the price agreed. He could also supply men to oversee what we were doing because we did not have

a clue. This company was building in the town I was living in, up
the street from where I lived. Now if that was not right, I did not
know what was.

Next week the delivery arrived but the lorry could not get up
the tiny road to the mountain. The materials had to be offloaded at
a local delivery base. The ICF was very light but it was awkward to
handle. From that base it had to be brought down the narrow road
to the site on a trailer, which took a full day. It was a day of gale-
force winds but we got it there eventually.

Two Polish men arrived the next morning to help us to get
started and stayed with us for three days. Jarlath had finished his
exams by this point and was helping too and very glad to get a job
for the summer. Brendie stayed in the stone cottage when he was
working, as did Noel, Tom, Kevin and any of the men who came
from a distance to work. It was great to spend so much time with
the boys and it was good for Jarlath to get to know them.

Jarlath was not the easiest to work with as he did not like his
mother ordering him about all the time so one day when things
got really bad I sacked him. He was mad but he was smart. He
apologised later and said, 'But you're my mother and you can be so
bossy on the site.'

'Jarlath, all the men on that site are my brothers and they're not
complaining. If someone is paying you to do a job you do what you
are asked, even if it's your mother paying.' So back to work he came.

The first floor was built and pumped with concrete and the
concrete floor was laid for the upstairs and to start the next floor.

Every year at this time we had a fundraising walk across the
Ox Mountains beside the house to raise money for the Gaelscoil at
home in Fermanagh, which Ruth and Seán were involved in. It had
never been held in Mayo before and all my family was staying in
the stone house or camping outside it for the night, Ruth's partner,
Wheaty, Dave and I were leading the walk.

By this time I had done some training in mountain leading
and I had my mountain skills qualification. I was at home in the
mountains and loved leading walks.

Seán was down as well and as we all stood on the concrete floor,
one storey high, looking up the mountains, he said, 'Christ, Mary,
this is so big you could land a helicopter here!'

Everyone laughed but I thought, 'I want no helicopter here!'

He reminded me of a time not too long before when I was out walking. A helicopter passed over and I jumped into the ditch, rolled into a ball and started to cry. I stayed there until eventually I pulled myself together and dragged myself back to the house. I was so shaken that I called a friend who lived across the road and knew what I was going through. I told him about the nights the helicopters came with the army and the police and someone was always taken away. When he left I was still so frightened that I asked him to leave his mobile beside his bed in case I needed him in the middle of the night.

It was the only time I had to ask anyone to be there for me in the middle of the night as I was so used to being alone. There was very little I could not cope with but I knew there was still something hidden deep, something I was very frightened of, something I feared was going to surface that night.

26

Help at Last

I got a feng shui expert to help me with the planning of the house: to have all the energies right in and around the house and the house positioned in the right direction. Her name was Elizabeth and I was a little afraid of her, probably because she reminded me of myself. My first engineer was not impressed! Elizabeth stood over him as he was drawing the plans on his laptop and was not taking no for an answer when he argued with her. I was delighted. She explained where the sun rose and set at the different times of the year and why it was so important to have the rooms in the right position.

Elizabeth is a lovely person, a direct, no-nonsense woman, the type of person I worked best with. In the course of our talks I told her a little about my background and one day she phoned me to say she saw a sign going into Enniskillen inviting people affected by the Troubles to call a Freephone number. I was delighted: for the first time I realised that there were other people out there who needed help and that someone had recognised this need.

I immediately called the number and heard that the service was only for people with physical injuries. I was devastated. I explained what I had gone through and that I had no physical injuries and the woman on the line said that I was not entitled to any compensation.

'I don't want compensation,' I said. 'I want to know I'm not the only person with all these problems. I want to meet someone who knows what I'm going through.'

'There are organisations that can help you,' she said. 'I'll send you a list.' And she did: a list of sixty-five organisations, the closest ninety miles away. It was too far for me to go to meetings so I continued the way I was, coping as well as I could and, apart from a few natural remedies when I hit a crisis, I continued using meditation, not medication.

I had planned that I would eventually go to live in the new

house in the Ox Mountains and run a business in the old one. Although there were two cottages it was really one that could function as two. This would be a retreat for people who wanted to get away from it all and have a taste of a more natural life, with good wholesome food, walks in the mountains and a little Tai Chi and yoga. And I would teach them to meditate.

I was under the illusion that I had got over my past. I talked to Dave and my sister Gertie about this (she was now a trained yoga teacher) and they both thought it was a great idea so I got my brochure together, had it printed and sent it to all the sixty-five organisations on the list. I wanted to meet some of these people involved so I thought I would bring them to me. I saw an opportunity to do a practice run on people like myself and get to meet them at the same time. Of course, deep down I figured I needed to save everybody else to save myself. I now know you have to start with yourself.

I got a response from a lady in Derry. She convinced the committee to that it would be good for the group she belonged to so we got the place ready and eleven people arrived from Derry. The two houses could not accommodate everyone so Mary, my neighbour, took in the overflow.

We had a great weekend and even though they knew nothing of my background I found out a little about theirs. I realised that I wasn't the only one with nightmares, flashbacks and anger. I also realised I was not able for this. It was too soon. I had a lot more work to do on myself before I could face anybody else's suffering. So I filed away my brochures and continued to help myself instead.

Now that the new house was started I had Elizabeth back on board and one day she came up to see me about the plans. She told me that a group in Dublin was helping people who had been hurt in the Troubles and that there was compensation.

'I know who you are taking about. You get compensation if you were injured in the North when living in the South.' I knew because Seán had got it. 'I don't want compensation, Elizabeth,' I said. 'I want recognition of what happened to all of us who have no scars to prove it.'

She gave me a number to call but I said, 'Elizabeth, there's no point. These people will not help and I'm sick to death of calling looking for help.'

The latest organisation I had phoned was Victims of Crime. It was as close to anything I was going to get in the Republic but they had no idea what I was taking about. When I was told they could not give me the name of the person who was going to help me – they would get him to call as they had to protect him – I knew I was definitely barking up the wrong tree.

'Call on Monday!' Elizabeth said as she left.

I had no intention of phoning that Monday morning but when I woke my wee voice told me to do it so I dialled the number and explained my case and asked if there was any help. When he asked if I was injured I wanted to scream and slam down the phone but I said, 'I have injuries so deep no one will ever see them.'

He answered 'I know what you are talking about. I'm from Armagh. We can't help you but I think I know someone who can. My name is Tony. Give me your name and address and I'll send you the information.'

I saw a little light but when few days passed with no letter I thought, 'You are like all the rest,' and put the whole thing out of my mind again. About a week later I got a note from Tony with a name and address in Dublin of a group called Justice for the Forgotten. I had no idea if they would be of any benefit to me but I thought they were aptly named.

I called and when a woman with a Dublin accent answered and said, 'My name is Margaret. How I can I help?' I felt like putting the phone down. How could I explain this again to a southerner who wouldn't have a clue?

I gave my name and where I got the number from and she said, 'What happened to you, Mary?'

I cried. All I could do was cry.

'Where are you from in the North?' she asked. She was trying to get some information out of me as I cried and cried.

'I'm from Fermanagh. Everyone thinks nothing happened in Fermanagh.'

'I know everything that happened in Fermanagh,' she said. 'Who are you? And where in Fermanagh are you from?

'My name was Lynch and I am from outside Lisnaskea.'

'You were beside where Michael Naan, Andy Murray and Louis Leonard were murdered,' she said and at this point I knew this woman truly understood.

'My brother, he was shot on the border.'

'Was your brother with Seamus McElwain?'

'Yes.'

'You are Seán Lynch's sister!'

I talked and talked and talked and she listened and listened and listened and nearly a hour later when I finished, she said, 'We can get you help, Mary. We have never been asked for help from anyone in Roscommon so I'll have to call you back with a name of a psychotherapist you can go to and we will pay for it. We are funded by the government to help people suffering from the after-effects of the Dublin and Monaghan bombings and northerners living in the Republic suffering from trauma.'

She called back half an hour later with a name of a woman in Westport. This was a long way from me but I did not care. This was someone who understood and I would have driven anywhere.

When I phoned the therapist she said, 'You are so far away. I can't expect you come this far.'

I assured her I would drive anywhere.

'No,' she insisted, 'I'll get you one someone closer.'

I had barely put the phone down when it rang again and the same woman said, 'My lecturer is one of the best trained in trauma in the country. He is married in Claremorris (which was only down the road from me) and he is from Derry.'

I called the number and made an appointment for two days later and that is when I first met Andy. At the first appointment I told him basically what had happened to me and cried for the hour. He listened with interest but before I left he said, 'Next week we won't be talking so much about what happened to you. We will be talking more about how it is affecting your life. You cannot live like this, Mary. You can bring it up again and again but what's the point? We could talk for forty more years and you'd be no better.'

'What do you think of him?' Dave asked, as we walked on the Sunday.

'Don't know.'

I felt that maybe he was dismissing what had happened to me but to be honest I did not want to talk about it any more either.

The next week Andy explained to me how he worked. He would listen while I told him about a particular incident. I would tell him how and where it was affecting my body. I knew I would have no problem doing this. 'Then,' he said, 'I will then show you some techniques that will help you to let it go.'

This is where I was having all the difficulties. I did not know how to let go. It was all going around and around and around.

That second week as we talked I said, 'Something in me trusts you.'

'Why do you say that?'

'Well, as I am taking to you, there is a thick black liquid pouring out of my chest into a big stone jar and that only happens when I'm around people I trust.'

'What do you do with the jar when it is full?'

'I bury it under a tree in my mind. It's a tree that I pass and sometimes sit under on my walk.'

'Who taught you to do this?'

'Nobody. I just do it because it gives me relief. When there is too much anger poisoning my body I drain it this way.'

He said, 'This is the way the Native Americans heal themselves. Did you ever read anything about them?'

'No. I just asked for help and this one of the answers I got. It worked so I continued to do it.' I never knew where the help came from. I did what my wee voice guided me to do.

Andy understood. He once said, 'What is happening to you is not normal, Mary, but it is normal for someone suffering from trauma.'

It was so wonderful that someone who understood. Dave helped me by listening but this man knew very well what I was going through. Andy had trained with people who worked with Vietnam veterans. He had heard it all before.

One Friday night at home, my body started to shake and I felt sick all evening and the next day. There was a terrible fear in me, an unnatural fear. As it persisted I meditated and asked my body what was wrong.

I knew then it was an old, old fear, a fear from my past. I called Mammy. 'When is Louis Leonard's anniversary?' I asked in passing, as we chatted about everything else. She is a very shrewd woman and I did not want to worry her.

'This weekend,' she answered. 'Why?'

'No reason. I was just wondering.'

I now knew what was bothering me and I could deal with it. My body would remember things that happened at different times of the year and this was one example.

Louis Leonard was a neighbour of ours who was found shot in the head in his butcher's shop the same year Dad's cousin and friend were murdered by the army. No one was ever charged or convicted but people suspected the army. It was another nail in the coffin that year when we buried our third neighbour and friend, brutally murdered.

Next week I told Andy.

'Yes Mary. That's what happens,' he said and he told me a story to explain: A man walks into a drugstore in New York at eight in the morning and with his finger under his jacket pretending to have a gun, he asks the owner to hand over his money. Being a wise New Yorker who has seen it all, the store owner knows that this man is not well; otherwise he would not be looking for money at that time of the morning when he has none, so he calls the cops.

This time they ask questions before shooting him. Back at the station they ask his name and when he tells it and his address they realise this is his third time he has been arrested on this date in the past few years.

'What do you do for a living?' they ask.

'I am a Vietnam veteran,' he replies, so they call his psychiatrist, who explains that on this day more than twenty years earlier he was waiting for a chopper to pick him and his friend up after all their platoon were killed. They were just getting on to the helicopter when his friend was shot.

Now I understood things even better. The body remembers and reminds you.

'But there is no need to dwell on this,' Andy continued. 'I'm only explaining why it happens.'

I found this fascinating. If you listened carefully your body would tell you everything you needed to know, in all kinds of ways.

Once I asked Andy, 'If you have a lot of trauma in your life, do you then need drama to replace it?

'Yes, Mary,' he said, 'for some people.'

That explained why, until I dealt with my past, I was always in the middle of building sites and business deals. I needed the drama.

Andy explained: 'If you are going down a street and see a man coming towards you, your body become aware of that man and you think, "Do I know him? Is he okay?" You are doing this all the time. Then your body prepares itself for this meeting. As you get closer you recognise who he is and it's not a problem so your body closes down to normality and you say, "Hi," and pass him by without a problem. In you have been traumatised, your body doesn't have the time to make these natural decisions so it opens up and does not close down. You are always on alert and nobody can sustain this level of awareness without causing themselves major problems.'

I was beginning to understand much more about my life: why I did things the way I did and why I was the way I was.

One Friday morning as I was driving to Claremorris to visit Andy, I was listening to Gerry Ryan, one of Ireland's leading radio broadcasters, talking to a childcare worker, Shane Dunphy, about the tiger kidnappings that were happening in Dublin at that time.

The expert described how this experience could affect the children involved if they did not receive immediate help. I was intrigued as he listed the possible outcomes. As he mentioned nightmares, flashbacks and addictions such as alcohol, drugs and work, I ticked off all the ones I suffered from.

It was only when Gerry said, 'We really don't have any experience of this in the country,' that I pulled my car to the side of the road and called his number.

When his researcher answered I said, 'My name is Mary Geraghty. I am forty-seven years old and was listening to your programme about the tiger kidnapping. I am driving to a psycho-therapist as we speak, suffering from a lot of the symptoms that are being spoken about on the show. I live in this country and I have experienced all this living here.'

'What happened to you?' she asked.

'I was held hostage with my family by the police and British army over thirty years ago and am able to deal with it only now.'

She asked if I would speak to Gerry and I did not hesitate to say yes. 'We'll call you back,' she said.

They called me back a few minutes later as I pulled in to park close to Andy's office. I raced to Andy's door as the show went into an advertisement break and told him I was about to be on the *Gerry Ryan Show* talking about my experiences.

For the next forty-five minutes I spoke about what happened that night and how it affected my entire life. I had no problem taking to Gerry and found him a really lovely gentleman, I was a little nervous; not about speaking to him or the fact that I was on national radio, but because I was afraid he might ask about my family and this was not about my family. It was about children who were traumatised. Really it was like talking to a good friend on the phone. At one point I could feel him about to cross the line into something else but he didn't and I was glad.

At one point I said to him, 'I remember looking out the window and seeing a house in the distance, one of the neighbours. It was five o'clock in the morning and the light went on and I was thinking it's a mile away, they will never see us again. And somewhere deep inside I blamed myself for being asleep.'

I also said, 'I waited for...for the gunshot, I think I have waited my whole life for it.'

It was much later that I realised that I had triggered another memory when I spoke of the gunshot.

Brendie was driving through Leitrim with his wife when he heard Gerry Ryan say, 'I have a woman in a psychotherapist's office in Claremorris who is going to speak to us about her experiences with a type of trauma.'

'That will be our Mary,' he said. And when I spoke he said, 'That *is* our Mary.'

It was great for me to be so open about all this on the radio as I knew my friends and family would hear the broadcast. There was a child in me that needed to tell her story but it was sparking off something I could no longer control.

A few weeks later I finished up with Andy so much better and so much wiser. 'I doubt if you'll ever need to come back, Mary, but you know where I am if you need me.'

'Do you leave many people to the door knowing they don't need to come back?' I asked.

'No, but you had a lot of the work done. You took me to the edge of my training and this is what makes my job worthwhile.'

'Thank you again for everything,' I said as I walked away. Little did I know that I'd be back to him before the end of that same year.

27

Trusting that All Will Be Well

After I finished with Andy I was feeling great and, even though things continued to come up, I was able to deal with them myself. He said to me before I left, 'This is never going to go away. You have to treat it like a bold child in the corner. Acknowledge its presence but don't let it overwhelm you.'

The house was up to the roof when I had to reapply for an extension of a year to finish it. Mary, my neighbour, had gone to England for a week so I was surprised when her sister called me to say a letter had come in Mary's name concerning the house and she thought it was for me.

'Read it out to me,' I said to Teresa.

It was about non-compliance with planning. It mentioned that I would have to close the site down and there was a fee of €12.7 million – not €12,700 – if it was not rectified! Teresa photocopied the letter and posted it to me.

I went to bed thinking, 'There is not much I can do now; might as well get a night's sleep.' Anyway, Dad and Mam were down with me and Mam was there to do the worrying if I told her. Now that the Troubles were over she was finding other things to worry about.

The following morning I got the letter in the post. I had not a penny to spare so I needed to get it sorted – and fast. My brothers were working on the house and I had no intention of sending them home unless I had no other option.

I called the county council and I asked as innocently as I could what the problem was so that I would have an idea of how serious it was. 'I think the house is too high above road level and something about the roof,' the girl said, 'but I can get the engineer to phone you. He's out at the moment.'

I left her my number and phoned Mark, my architect. He was

out of coverage so I got dressed and headed to the site. There was no point deciding what to say to anyone until something was said to me. I was pulling into the site when my phone rang and I recognised the county council's number.

'You got our letter,' a man said.

'I have it here in front of me.'

'The site is above road level and contrary to planning.'

'It is not. I had to spend €8000 to get it to where you wanted it and believe me, I didn't do that without carefully checking that I really needed to.'

'Let me check the map,' he said.

I waited and a few minutes later he said, 'You're right. You did have to raise it. But the roof is not in compliance either.'

This is what I had dreaded but hoped that we would have it finished before we would have to face this problem.

I said the first thing that came into my mind. I knew his name and used it. I had realised a long time ago that people, including myself, like you to use their names.

'Colin, could I explain?'

'Go ahead.'

'The plans I got were for a bungalow and I was never happy with it. I never thought it would look right in this scenic area, but at the time my major concern was for the old granary, which was to be gutted. So when we had to start the build the architect changed the plans to look like an old schoolhouse, which we thought would be more in keeping with the area. We had no time to submit another plan as the building had to be at roof level within five months of when we started, so even though I was losing floor space I thought it was a much better plan. The other fear I had was that it would look like a big bungalow that had fallen out of outer space into a different time zone.' I finished and waited.

'I think I know what you mean and if it is what I think I will have no problem with it. I have never seen it but will be out in the next few days. Get your architect to draw up a new set of plans and get them to me.'

'He has already drawn them; we'll send them in today.'

I had called Brendie on the way down to tell him what was happening. 'Shit!' was all he said.

The boys were working away when I got in to the house. Noel

was down now measuring for the roof. You could watch him work as he eyed up the house and within an hour he had all he needed written down.

I shouted up at them, 'I'll make the breakfast. I have it sorted.'

As I was walking down around the corner to where the stone cottage was, the phone rang and it was Mark. I told him the story. 'I'll bring the plans in today myself, Mary, in case we don't get him again.'

Back at the house I put on the bacon, eggs and sausages for the fry which was cooked about eleven every day after the boys had done a few hours of work. We sat down and I told them the story too.

'You're lucky,' Brendie said. 'I never thought they would come out.'

Luck has nothing to do with it, I thought. If you are doing the right thing the world has a way of helping you out. It just flows.

I had spent too long walking against the tide. If something did not work out, it was because it was not meant to and if it did work out it was because it was meant to. Simple as that, but I think we humans need complication. I used to too – but not any longer.

When I was at home that evening Mark phoned. 'I'm outside the county council offices and it's all sorted. The engineer even apologised that he would have to charge a fee of €500 but I won't charge you anything as it was my idea and, if I say so myself, one of the best ideas I ever had.'

'I agree, Mark, and it's the best €500 I'll ever spend.'

I meant it. The house would look perfectly in keeping with the area and we would have retention before we finished. All was well.

The wood was ordered, the roof started and more help was needed so we brought Kevin in on the job. Noel cut while Brendie and Kevin put the wood up and when I was there my job was to carry it in.

Noel, a very quiet man, shook his head at me a few times when I came out. 'What are those two boys talking about now? I never thought anybody could talk as much. You know I went up yesterday and they were in a deep conversation discussing whether the Americans ever really got to the moon.'

I laughed and thought to myself: isn't it great that politics are not the main topic of conversation any more – I'm not saying politics didn't come up but they were not the main topic.

The windows were to come in from Austria and the boys laughed again when I said I was getting them there. They laughed for no other reason than that they could not believe where I found the people I did.

I believe we are like the Internet, better than the one on the computer. If you want something you send your message out to the world, visualising exactly what it is. Then it comes and sometimes you might even get it on the world wide web.

I had always wanted triple-glazed windows, which no one was doing in Ireland at the time. I called everywhere and was told I didn't really need them – simply because they didn't have them. 'Maybe not, but I want them!' I would reply.

I was getting nowhere, so on to the computer I went and got the name of a company. I sent an e-mail and had a reply next day and a price within the week – cheaper than some double-glazed windows here.

I asked for references. The day Roisín finished college for the summer I picked her and her hundred bags up and we checked this supplier's windows out in five different counties.

Roisín would sit in the car if you drove around for a week. It was a good time to get all the news from her too so we had a great day. Even though building a house was not something Roisín had any interest in, she loved the fact that a bedroom that was going to be hers in Foxford, with a view overlooking the mountains and a window that was not about to fall out like the one in her bedroom at home.

Our home was nearly fifty years old but the reason her window was about to fall out was not its age but because she would open it with an iron bar in the middle of the night when she forgot her keys and could not wake me as I lay fast asleep with earplugs in my ears.

The day arrived when the windows were to come from Austria and a fitter was coming with them. On the way down Jarlath said, 'What if he has run away with your money, Mam, and does not come?'

'Well Ja,' I answered 'I did not give him that much money and I know he's going to come and they are going to be perfect.'

We were to meet the fitter in Foxford at ten but of course Jarlath had to stop for his daily supply of everything before we could move on – sweets, crisps, minerals and cigarettes somewhere at the bottom of the bag.

At five to ten the mobile rang to say the fitter was waiting and we got there a few minutes late.

'How come he can get here the minute he's supposed to coming from Austria and everyone else is late even though they're coming from up the road?' Jarlath asked as we pulled in to the site.

'This is Ireland,' I said. 'We do things differently.' The Germans had taught me how things should be done but I'd rather live in the west of Ireland where things are done differently, in their own good time, like the Bulmers advertisement.

The windows were in by the end of that day and looked as if they had always been there, like the windows in really old houses. I thought I would have to settle for windows that looked as if they had been replaced so I could have them triple glazed but again it was as if the Austrian had read my mind and they were perfect.

By this time the wood was all up on the roof and ready for the slates. The neighbours might have expected the Austrian to move quickly but I don't think they expected the boys to get the roof on so quickly. Noel and Kevin had now been working together a long time and each knew how the other worked, while Brendie slipped in and worked along with them as if he had always been there.

The slates came next and after much deliberating I decided on Brazilian slates, which were the closest I could get to Blue Bangors and a lot cheaper. I had put recycled Blue Bangors on the stone house but Elizabeth had advised me not to have old slates on a new house.

Up and down the roof the boys ran like cats. Everything was going so fast. We told jokes and different stories of our childhood. It's funny that so many people can live in the same house and have such different stories about the same incident.

We even talked about the Troubles but in a different way now. It was over, we were now free to talk and we were free in the wilds of the mountains of Mayo.

Roof finished and house sealed, we were now ready to partition the rooms off inside. How exciting that is, as you visualise where everything is going to be and, of course, change your mind all the time.

A few Polish men (friends of the men who helped us in the

beginning) had built the block walls, as we had no bricky in the family. Upstairs the partition walls had to be placed and I ran around with my tape measure trying to get all I wanted in and driving the boys mad. Like the dressing room I insisted I have, far more important to me than an en suite because I am not the tidiest of people. I wanted to see where my clothes were in order to wear them, instead of finding them years later lost at the back of the wardrobe after I had fallen out of love with them – and then having to give them away.

So my dressing room was measured out and I found I would have room for an en suite too. To live in a house that looked as if it had been there for ever but had all the conveniences of modern life is going to be heaven, I thought.

'The bath can be only four foot long,' Kevin said as he measured up, 'but then, Mary, you'll not have much problem fitting into that!'

'A shower over it and I'll be in heaven,' I said.

I was going to have a bathroom of my very own and, I hoped, plenty of hot water provided by the wind, when I could afford a turbine.

With the partition walls up I watched as the recession came in on us like a flash and all chances of my selling the stone cottage to finish the new house faded. It was to time to close down the site and wait with interest to see what would happen next.

28

Reunions

At the time we started building the new house my niece Joanna got married. It was Jarlath's seventeenth birthday and Roisín, Jarlath and I headed to Fermanagh for the celebration. It was the first of two weddings that year. Noel's son Kevin was to be married in Lanzarote later in the summer and most of the family was going there on their holidays and for the wedding. We all loved something like this when we could be together on a happy occasion.

There was a time, because of the war, that we did not stand in the same room for twenty-five years. Then we all met in a hotel south of the border for Mam's seventieth and Dad's eightieth birthday in 1998. Seán had got day release as his time was nearly up in Long Kesh and the peace process was in full swing.

All our celebrations were held south of the border then. Now Joanna was getting married in the local church and the reception was in the North, in the hotel where I had worked when it was bombed thirty years before.

Peter, her father, was the last family member to be married north of the border in 1981 and then in 1983 Seán and Geraldine got married in Clones within two weeks of each other. Gertie, the youngest of our family, was the last to get married. She had married ten years previously when tensions were high in the North and she too chose to marry in the Republic.

As the youngest member of the family, Gertie's first encounter with the British army was when the soldiers insisted in taking her out of her cot to search both her and it. That was the first raid and as the cot was no longer being vacated on a yearly basis for the next baby, Gertie lay for a longer time at the bottom of Dad and Mam's bed in that most precious place in the house.

Her early childhood days did not have the same freedom as ours did. The British army was always about. Only recently did she tell of a few instances of her contact with them. Once when she and Brendie (the youngest boy and her constant companion at the time) were playing in the wee hen house out in the haggard they heard a noise at the window and looked up to see a soldier there. He pointed his gun through the open space and without a word he released his safety catch as they huddled together, crying. Another time she rode her bike down to a neighbour's house and soldiers were lying in hiding in the ditch. They pushed a stick into the spokes as she rode by and she went over the handlebars. They laughed as she walked away, with blood pouring down her leg.

But the border was her big problem as her wedding approached. She and all the family was constantly being held there. Once she was held so long as she headed to a dance across the border with her friend that they had to turn back because the dance was over by the time they were let go. She was going to have to use the other way to get to her wedding.

The other way was by Lacky Bridge, which was one of the many border roads bombed by the British army so the locals were forced to cross by one of their checkpoints. This road was regularly opened by locals but bollards would be brought in by helicopter within hours to close it down again and there were so many bollards now it was nearly impossible to open it. Nearly but not impossible – as we found out the morning of the wedding when the males of both families and the best man used the digger bought for that very purpose (money raised by a dance) to clear a path for the family and friends going to the church.

I was not aware of any of this as I drove up to Fermanagh from Roscommon, crossing the border at Ballyconnell. I had to cross the border again to get to Clones for the wedding and I had been instructed like everyone else to cross at Lacky Bridge.

Brendie was there with his video camera and warped sense of humour as he took footage and commentated on the process. 'Come on, Peter, don't be afraid,' he said, as Peter carefully negotiated his way down the river to the southern side of the border. 'Maureen (Mam) has just passed through with no problem.'

Hours later when we were going to the reception and the road had already been closed again, the best man said, 'Well, we had to get out early this morning, so soon after Christmas, to make a path for the bride to get here and I have been wondering all day what I could call her. I thought maybe 'The Border Bride', but I decided on 'The Lacky Lady'.

Now, ten years later, we were free to enjoy ourselves on the Northern side of the border again. The hotel was much bigger than it had been but it was as beautiful as I remembered it. It was on its own grounds beside of Lough Erne, with the gardens going down to the lake.

The kids had a great time with their cousins, especially the wee ones. Some members of the family had a late start in producing children but there were now lots of wee ones.

I had never been in the hotel since I left in it 1978 but had no problem going there. I was feeling better than I had ever been in my life and we all had a wonderful day. The wedding was at the end of April, on the most glorious day you could ask for.

The kids and I drove home in the middle of the night. We chatted all the way back about everything and I told them stories about different members of the family as they asked questions.

I was still walking most Sundays, so next morning I was up and out, bright as a button as I had not been drinking the day before. When I was in the mountains I told the people who were walking with me all about the wedding.

'How did you feel to be back there?' Dave asked at one point.

'Not a problem,' I replied.

He knew as well as I did that it was not over but he also knew it was the one thing I would not talk about.

'Did they question you that time of the bomb?' he once asked.

'Yes, but I don't want to talk about it.' The tears would run down my face every time I thought of it. They still do.

'I'll go back there with you if you want,' he said. 'I will guide you there in a meditation and we can see what happened.'

The truth was, I could not face it. I said, 'No, I am never going there. I don't need to, nor do I want to.'

'We can bring Gary too and he will help you.'

When I was meditating now and needed to go somewhere I was afraid to go, I would bring two men with me for help. Even in my mind there were places I could not go alone, The two men I brought to protect me were Dave and Gary, my nephew who had been killed in New York. In fact I always carried pictures of them both in my pocket so that when things got really bad I could see through the tears and the darkness in my mind the faces of two people I had come to trust.

I sometimes thought in my saner moments that if I ever crashed the car and these pictures were found in my two back pockets, nobody would understand what they were doing there But I didn't care: I knew why and I knew I could trust them both.

But now I said to Dave, "No! I cannot, even if you and Gary are with me. I'm not strong enough."

Back in Roscommon I didn't think any more about the wedding day or the interview I had with Gerry Ryan the month before, but something had been triggered in me as I was having flashbacks again. Jarlath was doing his exams and I said nothing to anyone, not even Dave. I thought if I ignored them they would go away, for a while anyway. Jarlath was busy studying, I was busy with my new house and Roisín was back at college.

One Sunday not long afterwards, Dave and I were walking together. I was out of it. I was there in body only. I couldn't concentrate and when he produced the map as usual, I had no interest.

'I don't feel right,' I said as we were coming home. 'Something's wrong. Something's terribly wrong in me.'

'You'll be all right,' he said as he dropped me off but I knew that something awful was coming, I knew it. I had been in this place too many times before not to.

I went straight into the house, lay on a bed in the front room and stared out at the tall oak trees across the road, oak trees that were strong and leafy. I was weak, paralysed; I was alone as Roisín was not home from college that weekend and Jarlath was staying with his Dad.

The phone rang. I did not move, nor could I move. My mind was blank. I watched the light of day fade into the night and at some point I rose and crossed the corridor into my bedroom and fell into a bed that I knew I would find little rest in. I must have drifted off at some point as in the middle of the night I woke and I was petrified, I knew I could no longer hold on to it. It had surfaced after thirty years. I cried until morning and then sent a text to Dave: 'Please tell me that I don't have to remember what those bastards did to me.'

How I got out of that bed and drove to Foxford I have no idea, but I had to meet the boys and there were men to pay.

If anyone noticed anything when I arrived, no one said a word. I checked if they needed things on the site and then headed off as fast as I could.

I stopped the car in a lay-by on the way to Ballina and started screaming, something I hadn't done in a long time. There in the silence of the Mayo countryside I screamed and screamed, screams like those of a wounded animal that I had heard once before; screams I had held back for more than thirty years.

It was a very wet day and I stopped to wash my face in a puddle in the middle of the road as I went to pay for the stones that we'd got for the foundation. When I got to the office I just handed in the cheque and called the boys to say I had to go home.

All my life I had two memories that I would get from time to time to remind me of what I needed to remember but was not able to. One was off me standing at the side of the road outside the hotel, hysterical. The other was of my boss in the hotel telling me to go and wash my hair. I was always immaculate in my dress and could not understand this memory any better than the other one.

Dave texted to say, 'We'll talk tonight.'

On Monday evenings Dave ran a Tai Chi class in Donamon. I looked after the newcomers and took over when he could not make it or had another class. This worked out well for both of us as I loved to teach but didn't want the responsibility of my own class. We usually travelled together and had time to chat on the way up and down.

That Monday night when he came into the kitchen he knew I really wanted to talk to him because of the text that morning. 'We'll talk in the car,' he said.

'No, we'll talk now. I've waited all day to have this conversation. You know what is coming up and I want you to tell me that I don't have to face this.'

'Mary, you do have to face it,' he replied. 'You will have to go through it. There is no way around it.'

'I am not able. I am just not able to.'

'You are – or it would not have come up. You are strong enough for this.'

'No, I'm not.'

I was never one who avoided things but this was not just

anything. This was a dreadful memory that was forcing its way through me. We got into the car and there was silence on the way up and as he parked he said, 'You'll be all right.'

I did not believe him.

I had to leave the class that night and go into the toilet, where I cried in the cubicle.

Dave dropped me off later, assuring me that I would be fine but I knew he had no idea what he was talking about. He had no idea what it was like. How could he? He had not been there.

29

Waiting for the Right Time

I slept well that night, probably from exhaustion, and next day cleaned the house as if there was a demon in me. I thought maybe it would keep it away.

The following night I woke and I knew I could hold it no longer. It was the first time I could admit to myself that I was not only questioned by the police, I was tortured by them. Now that I had admitted it to myself I would have to face what really happened at the end of 1977.

I shook in the bed and let the few memories up – the fear of what they could do to me and what they had done to me. I shook and shook and sobbed and sobbed and released it from the centre of my being where it had been held too long and had poisoned my whole existence.

I just remember them taking me away in the back of a car. I did not want to go with them but I had no choice. I thought, 'What can they do to me? I know nothing.'

I called Dave's mobile, which I knew would be switched off, and as the memories came I just left messages telling him what they were. I did not need him to call me or be there; I just needed to say to someone what was coming so the next memory could surface, just like I did before with him. I had a terrible fear that I had been sexually abused and I needed to know.

As I left the messages and the memories continued I meditated on this and realised I was sexually abused verbally but not physically. There were things said to me that I could not say to anyone, not even a machine, so I wrote them down and burned them. I no longer wanted to carry them.

I continued to leave messages on Dave's answering machine about everything else over the next few days, assuring Dave that I was okay, that it was the only way I could release these memories.

I needed to tell someone and a machine was perfect. I needed neither interruptions nor questions.

We continued building the house and it kept my mind occupied during the day. I made it through the nights as best I could, exhausted from my work.

I remember talking to myself in my meditations and saying, 'I will deal with this, please give me time. Let me get this next wedding over and Jarlath off to college.'

I had done this so many times before and it did work. My body was now working with me and me with it.

A few weeks later one of my three remaining patients was taking into the psychiatric home as he needed more care. The next day Frank, another patient, went off to visit his sister for the weekend. I was alone that night with only one remaining man downstairs. It was the first night in over eighteen years that I did not have to assist anyone with their medication or anything else, I went to bed early and slept like a log.

Next morning there were a few messages on my mobile from Frank's sister. When I called her she told me Frank had stepped out in front of a car the night before and was in hospital but he was okay. But as I was leaving on the Monday morning to visit him, he died. I was very shocked as he had been living with us as part of the family for nearly nineteen years. One more gone and in my heart I knew I was being forced into a place where I would have no choice but to face things. I was being given time alone as it was only a matter of weeks before Jarlath was to start college.

It was the middle of the summer and Jarlath and I were going to the other wedding, this time in Lanzarote. Roisín wasn't coming as she had an allergy to the sun and could not go out in it without getting terrible headaches. I was looking forward to the break away from the site but was afraid of the burden of not having anyone to talk to and being so far away from the comfort of my own house and sanctuary. But I knew I could call Dave if necessary.

The memories had not stopped but they had slowed down and we went off to Lanzarote, where nearly eighty of us congregated in the sun for the week. I enjoyed it. I took walks on the beach and cried as I walked alone.

Of course, when we all got together we talked about the Troubles and one morning I went to visit two of the guests, two women from home who had seen more than their fair share of them.

One of them said, 'I heard you on Gerry Ryan, you spoke well.'

I replied, 'Peter said I said so much but I said so little. I know what he meant. Wouldn't Gerry Adams have been proud of me?

'What were you talking about?' the other lady asked, as she lit a cigarette,

I told her what I had spoken to Gerry about.

'What do you mean?' she said. 'I've been through so much but every time something happened I just put it in a box and locked it. I can't deal with that stuff. Don't tell me that I will have to open those boxes some day. I wouldn't be able.'

I know the feeling, I thought, but said nothing. I no longer had a choice.

With the holiday over, we headed back via Knock airport. Seán and Brendie dropped us off and Dad and Mam went home. They had been there yet again to mind my patients for the week even though Dad was now nearly ninety. As soon as they left I put on my rain gear and headed for my familiar walk to be truly alone for the first time in a week. I had only got around the first corner past my doctor Greg's house when I knew my body felt it had been more than patient with me and had done as I asked; it was now time to face it. I had a flashback of sitting on a bed with my knees under my chin trying my best to comfort myself. I now knew that I had been held for more than one day.

Dave and I walked together the following day. I told him about the flashback and before he dropped me off that day I knew this was something I would have to do alone.

Later that night I sent him a text: 'Don't pick me up tomorrow night for class. I am not going back or walking with you until I go through this, Thank you for all your help up until now.'

'What do you think he will reply?' my friend asked.

He will say, 'I truly understand.' Next day I got a message from Dave with those three words. I was alone. I needed to trust myself to get through this. How could anyone possibly know the pain of it? I was not able to verbalise it any longer.

Jarlath had started college in Galway the week before but was home with a bad chest, He had always had a problem with his chest – every winter since he was a child – and had been coughing lately, so when a neighbour told me about a faith healer she had been to, I thought it was worth a try. I made an appointment and brought Jarlath the next day. It was the day after I sent the message to Dave.

The man worked a little on Jarlath and then he said to me, 'Lie up on the couch and I'll check you out.' After a few minutes he said, 'There is a huge blockage in your heart chakra.'

'Tell me about it!' I thought.

'I'll work on it,' he said. He held my head and asked me to put my two hands over my heart.

When he was finished he said, 'You can come back to me if you want.'

'No, I can do this alone,' I thought.

He said, 'You may feel a little weepy.'

Jarlath went to college and I cried for the next six weeks. I cried when I was going to bed. I cried when I was getting out of bed. I cried everywhere. I cried in the car. I cried, I cried and I cried. Every moment I was alone I cried, until I wondered where all the liquid was coming from for all these tears and if I would ever be able to stop. It was as if a dam had burst again, worse than the first one, and the flood was coming through. Floods of tears would run down my face, even into my food as I tried to eat.

My friend said, 'Go back to Andy,' but I knew I could go nowhere until the tears stopped. After six weeks they subsided.

I was having nightmares and flashbacks as I remembered the events of the two days after the bomb. I would wake up crying, not knowing what would come next.

I remembered the policewoman I had mentioned only once to Dave in all the time I talked to him. One Sunday night years before, I remembered her in a meditation, I sent him a text: 'She was really a bitch, that policewoman.'

He texted back: 'You never mentioned a woman before.'

I replied: 'She was not a woman. No woman would do that to a child.'

I did not understand it at the time but now I did.

I remember being in a room with a policewoman and man. She was screaming at me, 'You know all about this, don't you. You know who did this.'

'No,' I answered, 'I don't. I never saw him before.'

'But you know who planned it, don't you?'

'No. I don't know anything.'

This screaming continued as I sat there and repeated, 'I know nothing,' as calmly as I could.

I was not going to cry. I had never cried in front of these people before and I was not going to now.

The man stood beside her and said nothing and all I could think was, 'He's all right. She's mad but he's all right.'

Maybe I wanted to believe he was all right but at one point he shattered my illusions when he walked over to the chair I was sitting on, lifted his boot and kicked it so hard that when I remembered it in my meditation. I could feel the pain go up through my right side as I landed on the floor. It was then I knew I might never get out of there alive: these were crazy people. I realised that they were capable of anything: I could see nothing but pure hatred in their eyes.

I was alone with them in that cell. I was trapped. No one knew where I was and no one would miss me. I was not due back to work for two days. The ones at home would think I had to work. The ones at work would think I was at home. I was a mouse in a trap and they had two days to torture me. Thirty years later when I told my brother he said, 'Why didn't you ask for a solicitor? You had a right to a solicitor.'

'No, Seán,' I answered 'I had no rights. They knew it and so did I. I was totally alone and they knew who I was and they were going to do whatever they wanted with me.'

It was as if the policewoman could read my mind and knew that I was hiding something, which I was.

One night before the bomb I was out at a dance in company and a man I knew said to me, 'You could easily bring a bomb into the hotel.' He pretended he was joking but I knew he wasn't.

'I would not!' was all I replied and I forgot about it, filed it away. Now I thought, as the policewoman screamed at me, if they found out from me. How would I tell? I would not tell. It was not that I owed him anything but I would not tell these people anything – any more than I would bring that bomb into the hotel.

I knew they were capable of doing anything. I knew things they had already done to people and I knew I was in a terrible situation but I also knew that even if I told them something they could dispose of me without a problem.

I just kept repeating, 'I don't know him. I never saw him,' which was the truth.

But it was relentless, as were the nightmares I had.

I went back to Andy and he taught me how to breathe through it. He said, 'Don't let it overwhelm you.' It was taking over my whole life – how could I not let it overwhelm me?

I went back a few times and he taught me other techniques for letting it go. He said I didn't really need to know what they did but I wanted to know. I needed to know what it was that forced me to leave home at eighteen and never return there to live.

Over the weeks I would remember a bit at a time, as if my body could only cope with a bit at a time. I would wake and I knew when my body was able to release a little more and I would trust that something would protect me. By now I knew that there are times you have to let go totally and trust, which is what I did. I had no other choice.

Like the night that I woke beating the blankets from around my head; I felt as if I was going to smother. I was petrified so I sat up and went into my meditation and asked to be shown what happened. I screamed as I remembered the bag going over my head and the rope around my neck. It was the middle of the night and I had no one to call. Even if I had, what could they do? I was back in the same situation as when I was in that cell. I had no one but my higher power to protect me and it did protect me as it had done before.

I sat there shaking and crying and visualised both Andy and Dave at the bottom of my bed as I let the memories and feelings come. They put the bag, a bag made of rough material, over my head from behind and put a rope around my neck and the policewoman kept screaming, 'What do you know?' I did not answer because I could not answer. I think this must have been the moment when I passed the fear of death. They will kill me anyway now. They don't care and neither did I any more. If I say anything I'm in trouble; if I say nothing I'm in trouble and they will probably kill me anyway. I did not care.

They told me I was lucky. I had three choices: twenty-five years in Armagh Jail; they would kill me; or they would tell the IRA that I told them who did it and the IRA would kill me. I thought of the community I lived in, the community I trusted, the only people I could trust since the soldiers came in that first night and I thought: if I don't have them I don't have anybody. If I can't trust them, I can trust nobody. I had nobody. I focused on the face of the man who had booked into the hotel and planted the bomb and I thought, 'I didn't know him. I know nothing,' and that became my mantra. I don't know how I knew to do this but, as I learned later in my life, when you have no help you know things instinctively.

Years later someone told me that they were trained to pick a spot on the wall and focus on it and say nothing if they were ever arrested. This is what I did but no one had every trained me. I focused on the face of the man who bombed the hotel.

Another night I woke up and I was back there in that cell again, sitting on a bed with my two legs up on my chest and my arms around them. I was alone. I was rocking and praying that they would come back and shoot me. I thought, if there is any mercy in any one of them they will just shoot me. I must have dozed off because the next thing I remember is the bed getting an unmerciful kick and I vomited. They pushed my face into it. It was relentless and so were the memories.

Then I remembered being calm, as if I wasn't there any more, as if I had left my body and watched as I was brutalised. I have no other memories of what they did. I didn't care. Nothing was ever going to be the same again if I survived and I had long passed caring whether I survived or not.

I have one other memory and that is of being in the back of a jeep with a crowd of men in uniforms with guns. They were all silent, it was dark and I was thinking, 'Which of them is going to shoot me?' I was not afraid. I had no fear of death.

They threw me out of that jeep. I was hysterical when they left. I did not know what to do or where to go. I did not expect to be left alive and I was not prepared for this. It was dark but not late and I didn't even know what day it was. This is what I wrote about night after night as the memories kept coming. I was angry and bitter and I tried to take it from my body and leave it on the paper, which I kept in the locker drawer at the side of my bed.

I hitched a lift and the man who picked me up had children in the car. I wept. He asked nothing. I said nothing. I have a memory of getting out of the car a few miles down the road but have no memory of how I got home from there but I must have make a decision on that journey to say nothing to anyone or to trust anyone. Somewhere on that journey home I blanked out everything that happened.

I knew I had to get away and shortly afterwards I went to Dublin. I was not functioning properly, That is when I started running and stopped trusting.

They told me I could not trust my family but that I could trust them (the police). The result was that I no longer trusted anyone.

They told me they would be back for me and I was afraid all the time. I believed they were capable of anything. I felt guilty about leaving but there was nothing else I could do.

I was not going to wait for them to return, I knew I would not be able for that again. I knew I'd never survive it a second time now that I knew what they were capable of doing. I still have no idea how long I was held. I lost all concept of time. All I know is that it was light when I was picked up and dark when I returned and it was not the same day. But I was there long enough to know that I could no longer live in this war.

I wrote this poem in the middle of the night when I woke from a nightmare. I remembered again sitting on a bed with my two knees up to my chest, knowing they were watching me from somewhere else and praying they would come back and shoot me.

I think I needed to explain to myself why I had that thought and why I understood so well that sometimes there are worse things than dying: there is living in a hell.

The Cell

One light, No air, so cold.
No peace, No break, No compassion.
Noise, screams, light, cold.
No morning, No noon, No night.
Water with salt,
Food on the floor,
Vomit in my face,
Eyes everywhere,
Hell on earth.

No wonder a bullet through the head was a welcome thought.

30

Moving On

Now that it was up and out I felt I had to prove it because no one would believe this. I could hardly believe it myself but it made so much sense in so many ways: why I left the North in such a hurry: why I would never return; why I had so many fears; why I am afraid to vomit. Any time I was sick I could never allow myself to vomit. I knew it would remind me of the last time and I was not ready to face that. Even a simple thing like why I could never wear a polo neck (I panicked as it was going over my head) and why I panicked in small spaces, especially when there were no windows.

I remember going into a storm shelter, an emergency shelter made of a waterproof material that we use for cover in the mountains. I told Dave I did not want to go in. As usual he said I would be fine but I was far from fine. I really panicked when the cover went over our heads, even though he left me beside the vent. I did not want to cause a scene as there were about eight of us in it, but I said, 'Dave if you don't stand up and let me out I will cut the side of this to get out.' And I really meant it. One Christmas the children got me a present of a day in a spa. It was in a beautiful place but when I went for my massage I found that the room had no windows and my heart was thumping. I had to visualise my friend's massage room to stay there. When the masseur was finished and left the room I put on my dressing gown with my eyes closed and I got out of that room more quickly than I ever got out of a room in my life.

I tried to get my medical records because I remember going to the doctor with a pain in my back and right hip and I have always had a problem with my right jaw.

I remember the doctor asking me, 'What age are you?'

When I said eighteen she said. 'How could you have a pain in your back at eighteen? What do you want me to do, call

Burnhouse?' Burnhouse was the name of the people you called to have your animals put down.

I think I may have thought of telling the doctor that day, my own doctor, who was lovely. We were never brought to doctors as children – all was cured at home – but I used to play with her children when I stayed in my friend's house in town and she was always nice to us. But as she was not there, I never told anyone.

I knew those medical records would have the date I went for help after the incident but a year later when I finally traced them to the vaults of a office in Belfast, they had lost the records for the first nineteen years of my life.

Eventually I had to trust that I knew what happened to me and if no one else believed me I didn't care.

I knew this was it. There may be more to emerge about that time but I knew that this was what had changed my whole life and now I had to let it all go. With Rosin off to Canada for the summer and Jarlath working near home and driving my car most of the time, I had time again to be alone and to let go.

Jarlath had been driving the summer before and I took him off the insurance when the government decided to enforce the law that learner drivers had to have a qualified driver with them. When they changed their minds two days later I did not change mine and he was not a happy camper. 'I'll put you on my insurance when you get a date for your test,' I told him. That will encourage him to do it, I thought. There are enough learner drivers on the road. I thought right because he passed it early the next year before he was eighteen and then proceeded to take my car as if he had a better right to it than I did – a bit like the bathroom!

I really had no problem with his having the car because it meant that I walked even more and kept on trying to come to grips with what had happened to me. I took the summer off and with only one patient left downstairs I had the time. I could say the world cleared the decks for me. I was grounded. I knew it and I went with it.

In the years since I left the church and stopped feeling that pull to go back, I had come to find a God that I had always known was there, a God of love. He did not think of me as better than anyone else. He did not think of me as worse than anyone else. I was as much a part of him as he was of me and now we were working very well together.

I had my problems with him in the past. How could he be so different in so many different churches? How come some people thought they had the one and only true God? That they had a better right to him than anyone else? That he loved them more?

I did look at other religions and I could honestly see no difference when you got to the bones of them. They thought they were special whereas I believe we are all special. So I decided I would love the God I had found and share him with everyone else, and that is what I do.

I have two children and I love them both. I have very different relationships with them and that changes all the time but how could I love one more than the other? I do for each of them what they need help to do. The other may be perfectly capable of doing whatever that is but needs help with something else, so I help as best I can with that.

Not that for one moment do I think I know better than either of them about their journey on this earth but, as I tell them, sometimes I do understand things just because I have lived a little longer.

I figure my God is like that: he gives me the help I need when I need it but also gives my neighbour the help he or she needs and loves us both equally. Maybe you think I'm simple-minded – maybe I am – but it works for me and I'm sticking to it. I need no organised religion, nor do I have a problem with any one who does.

I must say I had to fight to get here and most of it was done with God. I once walked in the mountains alone and broke a walking stick as I battered the turf bank and screamed at him: 'Why do you complicate things so much? Why do things have to be so difficult? Why do you have so many rules and regulations, so that I don't whether I'm coming or going?'

'I don't,' he answered, 'you do.'

Whatever situation I was in it was for a reason; I found the reason was usually for growth, my growth. I remember a spiritual healer (I'd been to everyone before I got to me) once asking me, 'What you think you have to learn?'

'To love myself,' I replied without hesitation.

'Well you picked a great place to be born,' she said. 'In the middle of a family of twelve and into the middle of a war!'

How often I think of that and how true it is.

I had learned so much and the most important was to love myself. Loving everyone else became easy then.

I learned it but it was not an easy lesson as I thought of the bastards who tortured me.

I would go into my meditation and think of them. I think I had forgiven the soldiers by then but not the police: these were the people we were encouraged to trust.

I would go there and think: why?

I was not ready to let go yet but I knew I would find a way when I was ready – and I did.

It reminded me of the time I thought I had told Dave everything and he said, 'Well you know what you have to do now.'

'Of course I know what I have to do,' I snapped. 'I have to let go but it's been with me for such a long time I want to hang on to it for another wee while until I'm ready.'

It was now time to let this go.

I had started practising Tai Chi on a Saturday morning with two neighbours I had trained with and was not surprised when Padraig came with a book one day and said, 'You should read this because you could have written it.'

He was right because the woman who wrote the book had worked with her illness exactly the same way I had.

The organisation was training people to work with others in order to heal their lives and I called their London office. When she told me the price to train I thought, 'It's not for me. I'm doing this already myself and I'm not paying anyone that kind of money to get a piece of paper.'

I was never a lover of those pieces of paper that said someone else had told you how to do something that you knew perfectly well how to do yourself if you took the time to listen.

I was about to hang up when she said, 'If you give me your e-mail address I'll send you the names of our practitioners in Ireland. They're looking for case studies to finish their course.'

A few days later I got around to calling numbers. Only three were within forty miles of where I lived and I would need to borrow my car from Jarlath to get to one of them.

I rang the first number and I left a message. A woman answered the second and she told me she was moving abroad within a week. She wished me luck, as I did her.

The woman on whose answering machine I had left a message got back right away and I made an appointment to see her. She was Australian and a lovely woman. I told her what I had done myself and that it was just what they were doing. We understood each other very well as she brought me into where I had been going myself for years. Mine was the Irish version; she was working on the American version and talked about campfires. I told her I went into a room with an open fire.

Of course the police were on the number one spot. It all went well until she said I was allowed to say what I wanted to them, which I did with pleasure, but then I was to listen to what they had to say in return. I had also done this before but I did not want to hear what these people had to say. Today was not my day to listen. It was great to be reminded of what to do but there is a process and there is no point pretending you can forgive when you can't. It just does not work.

I got another appointment and rushed home with the car to Jarlath and went off for my walk.

I was still doing the same route and now knew everyone living on that circuit through the countryside – not that I got to talk that often to them. I often wondered if they had any idea of what I was doing in my head? I ranted and raved on those walks and cried and cried but I doubt if any one noticed. As my friend Marita said about me, 'You could cry for five hours and nobody would know five minutes later that you had shed a tear.' She knew because I often drove down to her after I had done precisely that. Hers was one of my safe houses at that time (still is), a house where I can go and cry when I can no longer cope alone. She would put her arm around me and encourage me to let it out, to feel the fear and then let it go.

A few mornings after being with the therapist I woke up and knew I had to do a meditation. I always know now. It's like knowing when to eat and if both cries come together I would meditate. For me the cry of the soul has always been stronger than that of the stomach.

I sat cross-legged on my five-foot bed. I could lie on it whatever way I wanted and still be within its boundaries. It wasn't any easier going there now but by now I knew the procedure very well. I sank into myself and who was there but the crowd from that cell, that hell, that interrogation room or whatever it was? I was no longer afraid. The process I had followed with my gut for the previous years had worked. It was a slow process but such a very deep wound took time to heal.

It was time to forgive but not before I said my piece again and took great pleasure in.

'I was only eighteen,' I said, 'a child – even though I thought I knew it all and had seen too much. I didn't need this brutality, which forced so many people to retaliate. I had already seen enough and was not going there, even though I understood why people did. It was not part of my journey. I lost everything during those days – everything that you had not taken before. I lost the ability to trust. You had taken my home years before.'

One of them (the woman) replied, 'Well, this was also part of your journey.'

I felt like hitting her, even though I knew she was right. She said, 'We too had our causalities. We had friends killed.'

'Yes, I know, but you chose to join your organisation. You were paid. I was a child and I was involved in nothing.'

While I was writing this book I remembered in a meditation that a policeman was shot dead about a mile from where I was brought up at home. I checked it out on the RUC website and realised that it was the same year they tortured me and that he was the same age as me.

The day he was shot I was in a town in Tyrone staying with a Protestant family. I was going out with one of their boys. I was watching the TV with them and didn't flinch when the news flash came through even though I knew our house would be destroyed by the police that day. Forgiveness took another while but it did come and I found the company of the Australian lady on this last bit of the journey comforting. I had been a long time working on this alone.

The summer ended. Roisín returned with all the tales of Toronto and the loss you always feel when you leave something you loved. 'It's a chapter in your life, pet,' I said. 'You will always have good memories of it and maybe some day you'll go back.'

'I will,' she said, and I thought of Germany and all the promises I had made to return.

As both she and Jarlath were getting ready to go back to their colleges, I was having sweet dreams of getting my car back.

I loved when the kids went to college and they would phone home to ask how to do the things they had taken so much for granted. With Roisín it was about cooking at the beginning. Jarlath could cook but Roisín's idea of cooking was pouring the milk over the cereal. She was the cleaner, which Jarlath did in spurts. His room was a bit like Fagan's bedroom with clothes all over the floor and bed. Roisín's was immaculate; she was organised.

One Saturday morning, as he came up the hallway still half-asleep, Jarlath asked me, 'What time do the banks close today?'

'They don't open on a Saturday,' I replied. I was smiling but I really had to laugh when he continued, 'When did they stop opening on a Saturday?'

They learned to appreciate the comforts of home. Roisín would call from Athlone, on her way home from college, to ask if I had anything for dinner. I was only too glad to cook now that it was not an ongoing chore and I then had the pleasure of watching them wolf it down and appreciate it, especially Roisín, who loved to be fed, like her mother. Doesn't a little appreciation go a long, long way? All the way to the cooker in this case.

Jarlath was not happy to be going back to college without a car and one morning he told me of the plan he had come up with in the middle of the night, when he couldn't sleep, to be able to afford his own car. He would move out to the suburbs of Galway, where rents were cheaper, get a job and apply for a loan to buy the car.

It wasn't a bad plan and it was what he wanted so he and I set to work on bank loans (that is after the one from me to bridge it) and insurance, with Granny worrying, but it was all part of the cycle, the learning, and I went along with it – not that I had any chance of stopping him. I had spent too much time trying to stop things that I couldn't stop.

So off to the North we went and bought the car – it was a lot cheaper there. He got the loan and insurance and learned another lesson rapidly: when you get a loan the repayments come out of your account every month. So he got a job at the weekends.

I got my lovely car back. It was a silver Golf. I adjusted the seats and the steering wheel and everything else he had moved and dumped the air freshener into the bin.

The new house was at a standstill because of the recession and I was at a loose end. It was time to move on.

I wrote: 'Today, 7 September 2008, I totally let go of the illusion that I have any control over anything or anybody. I surrender to a power greater than me with no conditions. I surrender all my possessions, all my attachments, human, animal and material, as I let each day take care of itself. I open up my life to a new career or job or relationships and I let go of any need to control any of them. I trust my higher power with my life and my needs and thank the guidance you have given me in the past forty-nine years as I have struggled to get to this stage. I thank you for everyone in my life I have learned from and let them all go with love and thanks, no matter what the lesson was.

'I feel a peace in me now that I have never experienced before and I know I shall have it until I leave my body in this life.

'I have struggled so hard to hang on when all I ever needed to do was to let go and *trust*.'

31

STARTING OVER

'I'm going to train as receptionist,' I said to Dave.

He laughed. 'You are not going to be a receptionist again!' he said, but I knew I had to do a receptionist's course as it kept coming up in my meditations. I was soon to find out why.

I had very little contact with Dave in that year since I finished Tai Chi, I had spoken briefly to him once in Foxford when I was working and he was walking there and I had texted him when the new group I had joined were going to climb Carrantuohill, a mountain we had both always wanted to climb, and he said he would love to come along. With all this time alone I figured I would have gone through a lot of the process before we met again – which I had.

When we headed to Kerry on the bus, about forty of us, we chatted like two long-lost friends and each brought the other up to speed on where we were. Dave was far from being a businessman and I had long since given up telling him how to run a business. I smiled as he told me of his latest ventures and I told him of the year that had passed. Time never seemed to make any difference to our friendship; it flowed naturally.

We had a fantastic weekend and met up again a few weeks later, as we were both leading walks for the voluntary development organisation, Bóthar.

When I want to do something I'll tell everyone. I always get a lot of advice, most of it no good, but then there is always one person who knows. My friend Anne Keegan said, 'You should go on a FÁS course.'

'I'm not allowed on those courses,' I said. 'I'm self-employed.'

'Call them!'

The lady who answered the phone told me there was a receptionist's course starting in the next town the following

Monday and that I might get a place so off I went to meet the organiser. I missed her by about two minutes but was given a number to reach her.

I called it and was told that she would not be back that day but to call in the morning. I did and she said, 'That course is full and has a long waiting list.'

I said okay and thought it was simply not for me but she said, 'I'll send you out an appointment and you can sign up with us. Maybe something else will come up.'

A few days later I got an appointment and headed down to meet her. She wasn't there. I checked the appointment and I had got the wrong date so off home again. The following Thursday, on the right date, I wasn't going to go because I was getting rid of the windows in my house that were now about to fall out. They were single glazed and all my heat was going right out through the holes in the frames and the panes of glass.

I could not afford new windows but neither could I afford not to get them as I was getting triple glazing at cost price. My new Austrian friend made this offer to me because I had sold so many windows for him. So that Thursday I had an Irish company fitting the windows because the lone Austrian fitter could not keep up with the orders. Maybe I should have looked for a share in the company!

The wind was whirling through the house from every angle as I took off to see the lady from FÁS. I hadn't even changed my clothes as I was beginning to think that I was not meant to meet her but there she was.

'What do you want to do?' she asked, as I filled in a form.

'I want to start that receptionist's course that started two weeks ago in Ballagh, that one that is full and has a waiting list,' I said with a smile.

'Well, can you start on Monday morning?'

That's when the doubts started as I wondered how I would get time for my latest venture, importing cars from the North, (it seemed like a good idea after I imported Jarlath's and I saw an opportunity).

'Just do it,' said my wee voice.

'Okay,' I said to the lady from FÁS, 'but will I be able to catch up?'

'No problem!' she answered. 'And there is another Northern woman starting with you.'

'Who?' I asked

'I can't give that information. It's confidential. Bring your bank details,' she continued.

'But I won't get paid, will I? I'm still technically self-employed.'

'Bring them,' she said. 'Everyone gets paid to do a FÁS course.'

As I left I realised that my mortgage would be covered until Christmas and I was going to learn more about computers so I could get a job. Brilliant!

So off I went on Monday morning to start my new course to retrain as a receptionist.

I knew this town well as I passed through it many times going to Foxford but had to ask for directions as I never knew this side-street existed. I left early and arrived early and I recognised the northern number plate and knew it was my buddy who was also starting this morning.

I always liked to see a northern plate in the west; it made me feel there was someone who understood.

Out I got and straight over to the car. A woman was getting out.

'Hi. I'm Mary. Are you starting the course this morning?'

'Yes, I'm Joan.'

As we went through the main door and up the stairs we spoke to the other women who were two weeks ahead of us and they gave us the run-down on what was going on.

I found I had an instant bond with Joan; maybe because she was from the North or maybe because she was new like me but there was certainly a connection, even though before we reached the classroom I had found out she was from east Belfast and surmised she was from the 'other side', as we say in the North.

We got to the classroom and the teacher welcomed us. 'Another Englishman!' I thought, as he introduced himself, but this was no longer a problem for me. It was at times like this that I knew how well I was. It was as if something in me was checking me out. 'Well, check me out,' I thought, 'this is something I have overcome.'

'We'll sit together,' said Joan but all the computers were taken and we were separated to different sides of the room, which was to prove interesting.

Dominic, the teacher, told us what we would be doing but most of the morning was spent filling up endless forms for FÁS. I was beginning to get a little nervous. It seemed everything was being done on the computer and I was far from being computer literate, whereas Joan was already a secretary. My only experience with the computer was teaching myself while asking questions of two impatient teenagers. They would look at me in horror at how little I knew, as if people were born with these skills.

At tea break Joan and I got together and chatted about why we were there and general things. Everyone else assumed she was a Catholic – everyone always assumed you were a Catholic in the west because up until recently ninety-five per cent of the people there were Catholic.

Lunchtime arrived, none too soon, as it was years since I had sat for so long, four hours in a seat. It was now more than twenty-five years since I had done a start-your-own-business course in Galway and nearly thirty-five since I left school and went to the university of life or, as it's sometimes called, the university of hard knocks.

It was a beautiful October day and we went outside and sat on a wall across the road to eat our lunch in the sun.

I had been living in the west for nearly twenty-three years by then but it was not long since I had started to be open about my background. Things had changed, I had changed and I had come to realise that if someone had a problem with me, it was their problem. After opening up to Dave I had started doing the same thing to others. At first I waited for their reaction; now I didn't even notice.

I tested this out in the mountains when people were relaxed and open.

But this was different. Joan was different. We started to talk about the North as I could see she was like a fish out of water here. 'You know,' she said openly, 'I am not a Catholic.'

'Neither am I any more but I come from a Catholic background, not only Catholic but Republican to boot. We both laughed and talked about the North as it were a foreign country, which a lot of people consider it to be, on both sides of the border.

By the end of that first day I thought I would never catch up on all the work but I soon did.

This course, I learned, was to get people (all women) out of the house and back into a routine of going to work and to instil the confidence in them to go out and get a job.

As the week passed, Joan and I gelled and we bantered across the room about things we understood and the rest got to understand. Joan was in the class by default – or so she thought. She had ended up living in the west when her job and her partner's job finished in England. The only home they had by then was a holiday home in the west and she was doing the course and deciding what came next. She was very much like myself and we thought alike. You are never in any situation unless there is a reason and I was very soon to learn one of my own reasons for being there.

Dominic had told us at the beginning that a CV had to be done and how to do it. 'If you have one already at home,' he said, 'bring it in and we'll go through it.'

Teatime came and when we got to the kitchen Joan came over to me with a very worried face, which was unusual for her as she was such fun, the life and soul of any party.

'Mary, I don't know what to do,' she said seriously. 'I don't want to bring in my CV.'

'Why?'

I don't want anyone to know where I worked.'

'Why?' I answered, smiling. 'Did you work for MI5?'

'No. I worked for the police.'

That's all she said, 'I worked for the police,' and I froze inside. I completely switched off but in a second answered her, 'Just tell Dominic. He'll understand. It's no one else's business and anyway Joan, nobody will care.'

No one but me, was what I was saying.

We went back to the computers. I know very few people will understand how I felt. A fear had started to shut me down. I couldn't see the computer and I couldn't work. This woman was a typist, a simple typist, and in the past two weeks I had really come to like her but the thought that she typed for those people hit something in me that was never going to go. I had completely closed down before I left that afternoon.

How could such a simple thing knock me back so much?

Andy had said, 'You know, it will never go away Mary. You will have to learn to live with it; it will be triggered. But whatever you do, don't let it overwhelm you.' I had done just that.

I cried all the way home as memories surfaced again of the people I thought I had forgotten and forgiven.

I could not eat that night. I didn't answer the phone. I made one call to my friend, Anne, to whom I talked most days. I didn't want her to do anything but listen – and she did.

I cried myself to sleep and had nightmares again.

The next day was Friday. I didn't want to go back but we finished early on a Friday so I decided I would go, Crossing the narrow, crooked bridge that was on the way into town I scraped the side of my car because I could not judge the width. I was not fit to drive. This was something that had happened to me regularly over the previous few years, after nightmares or flashbacks. I was shaking when I went in and left shortly afterwards, telling Dominic I was sick.

I *was* sick. I went home and to bed and for the first time in over a year I called Dave with a problem and left a message on his mobile. I was crying.

'Dave,' I said, 'there is a woman in my class from Belfast and she worked for the police as a typist. She was only their typist and I really like her. I am shaking and I can't stop crying and I can't eat. What is wrong with me? Why I do have I go through this again?'

He phoned back and said, 'Remember what Andy told you. This is not going to go away. It's like a bold child in the corner. Acknowledge its presence but ignore it.'

How could I ignore it, I thought, as I cried myself to sleep again? I thought it had gone away. I thought I was over it.

That night I remembered what they said to me. 'If you tell anyone we'll kill you all, starting with your mother.' I knew they were capable of doing it.

I had remembered those words all my life but told people they were said to my brother Kevin. Now I realised that they were said to me too.

I told Jarlath I was sick and stayed in bed most of the weekend, Roisín was not at home.

On Monday morning I went back to class. When I got there, Joan was one of the first in and she was alone in the corner. I went over to her and told her what had happened to me when she told me she worked for the police. She put her two arms around me and said, 'I'm so sorry, Mary.'

'It's not your fault. It is something I have to deal with and will always have to deal with.'

I never did tell her what happened to me.

By the end of the week I had settled down a little and decided to go walking on Sunday with another group to get out in the fresh air and ground myself.

32

IF IT FEELS RIGHT, DO IT

After I had finished walking with Dave the year before I stopped walking on the mountains for a few months and I was lost without them. One day I was in Dublin shopping with Roisín when my mobile rang and I saw Tom's name come up. Tom and I had trained in the mountains together.

'Hi, Mary,' he said, 'we're walking in Foxford this weekend. Do you want to come with us?'

A spark lit in me and I said, 'I'd love to but I can't. It's my uncle's anniversary Mass and I want to go.'

'Do you mind if we park our cars outside the stone cottage?'

'Not at all. Will you do me a favour and call me when you are walking again?'

'No problem,' he said and hung up.

Two weeks later he phoned and said, 'We're walking on Sunday in Cuilcagh. Do you want to come?'

'Yes please!'

'Meet us in Boyle at ten.'

I loved being back in the mountains, the big open space, the tough climbs, the fresh air, the companionship, the chats. We had lunch on the side of the mountain with the sun shining down on us. It was wonderful to be back.

On the way down I made a decision. I walked up to Tom and asked, 'Can I join your club?'

'No problem,' he replied. 'That would be great.'

I had walked with them for nearly a year now and as they walked every second weekend I had got into the habit of joining other groups on the alternate Sundays if I wanted to get out. This was one of those Sundays and I called around to see where everyone else was walking and set out to meet a group.

I was not the only one who did this. You could meet anyone

anywhere, and there were a few blow-ins like myself that day. Jack was there, another Englishman. I was beginning to think they were wearing a path to me but had no problem with any of them any more.

The week before, another group was doing a one-day course downstairs in the building where my course was being held. As I passed through the group to the microwave, to heat up my soup, a piece of paper hit me on the ear. I turned around and there was John.

John was a friend of Dave's (English too), who was practising Tai Chi when I first met Dave. He would constantly pick on me and could rise me very easily. I never knew what it was about him that niggled me but I later realised that at that time I found it nearly impossible to be in the company of two Englishmen at one time.

Well, that day I smiled, walked over to him and said, 'How are you, John?' and gave him a hug. He really was a lovely man and the problem was all mine and now it was gone. We chatted and I left him, knowing I had let go. I had conquered another problem.

Jack was a middle-aged man who, like myself, took to the mountains for peace. I felt he was a troubled soul, which is probably why we got on well together. We would talk about all kinds of things and of course I had brought up the North on a number of occasions and I knew he understood. I was surprised about how much he knew and understood and put it down to the fact that I suspected he was a Republican sympathiser. I said this to him later and he said, 'I am.'

That Sunday I was very vulnerable after the week I had just had in class with Joan. I was telling Jack a funny little story, about an incident in class. One of the woman had asked me to lend her a little tape recorder I had but when I took it down from the top of the kitchen press, I realised that the interview with Gerry Ryan was still on it I had taped it from the Internet that night I had spoken to him. I didn't have another tape and was trying my best to clear it.

Jack interrupted me and asked, 'What were you taking to him about?'

'Post traumatic stress. I suffered from it because of the Troubles.'

'So did I,' Jack said.

I couldn't believe it! He was the first person I had ever met who admitted that he was afflicted by the same condition as me and I was so glad to meet him. For years I thought I was the only one.

I looked him straight in the eye and asked, 'What happened to you?'

He said without hesitation, 'I was a British soldier in Northern Ireland.'

I don't know which of us was most startled: he who said it and turned a lighter shade of pale or I who just heard it and had no reaction.

His eyes filled with tears as he tried to compose himself. I wanted to reach out to him but didn't. He was very upset. 'I can't understand why I told you,' he said. 'I have never told anyone else. Some of my family don't even know.'

I knew by this time that his father was Irish.

'I cannot sleep at night. I think it's my penance for the things I did there. I will never forgive myself.'

The rest of the group had wandered on and nobody noticed what was going on behind them. I always lead walks from behind so we were at the end of the group.

He talked and shook and my heart went out to him. I knew exactly what he was going through. It did not matter to me that he belonged to what I had considered the enemy for most of my life. I had met a fellow traveller in a place you would not wish your worst enemy.

We talked and talked and I said, 'You have to forgive yourself. You can't live like this. I now know I have no problem forgiving you. It was a war. You were young and this was part of your journey to learn whatever it is you need to learn.'

As I drove home that evening I could not believe what had just happened and how I had dealt with it. How I could reach out to a man who was a member of a group of people who had traumatised me, for whom I had held hatred in my heart for most of my life? It was gone!

Maybe I still had problems with the police but the army had evacuated my body. I remembered doing a meditation and watching the army withdraw from my body. Now I realised they were truly gone.

Jack and I decided we would meet again the next week and over the coming weeks we talked more but I watched as he shut down again. He might never be able to open up again. I hope for his sake he can, as the alternative to facing it is the long slow torturous death of your soul.

I gave him my number and told him to call me if he needed anything but I never saw him again. I only hope our meeting did as much for him as it did for me.

Later that night I texted Dave and told him. He texted me back: 'Be very careful.'

I returned: 'I no longer need to be. I had no problem with him. He had a much bigger problem with me.'

I could just imagine Dave smiling when he received it.

There was a woman called Mary in my class with whom I had become very friendly. She was a Dub who had brought bag and baggage and come down with her husband and kids to live in a home they had bought in Roscommon. The week before in class when I was trying to get myself together after what happened with Joan she had shouted across the room, 'What was your maiden name, Mary?' and as I was in a state of paranoia at the time, I was nearly afraid to answer. I walked over to her and said, 'Lynch.'

'Mine too!' she answered.

Dominic had told us to mention our hobbies on our CVs.

'Can I put down walking?' I asked

'Not unless you're a hill walker.'

'I am a hill walker.'

'That's good. If you have any training put that down as well.'

At the tea break Mary came over to me and said. 'Would you mind if I came walking with your group some time? I've always wanted to do it but never had the courage to go on my own?'

'We've grade A walks coming up but I'll take you to the Ox Mountains some Sunday and see how you like it and then you can join us if you want to.'

We went with another woman in the class in tow and Mary joined our club. When we went out I told her about Joan. I wanted someone to know what was happening if I could not cope. We decided if it overwhelmed me again I would say I was sick and ask to go out for a walk and she would get up and come with me. She was my backup and even though I never needed it, I was comforted to know she was there.

Geraldine (another Dub who had married a local man) was a great seamstress and when I told her I had bought a dress in

London two years before but didn't like the length of it, she said, 'Bring it in and we'll see what can be done with it.'

She altered it and I had a new dress to wear.

Geraldine was also full of information about everything, even though she never gave herself enough credit. One day as I was practising my typing, I was sitting beside an eighteen-year-old. Even thought we didn't have a lot in common I understood eighteen-year-olds a little as I had one at home.

'April,' I said, 'I had a dream about snakes last night.' I was really taking to myself. 'Who, I wonder, would know anything about dreams?'

I looked around the room. Geraldine and Joan were sitting together so off I went and stood between the pair of city woman from the two sides of the border who were bosom buddies now.

'Anyone know anything about dreams?'

'No,' Geraldine answered immediately but continued, 'What did you dream?'

'I dreamt that a huge snake was crawling up my body.'

'Are you afraid of snakes?'

'Terrified!'

'Were you afraid of the snake in the dream?'

'No.'

'What did you do in the last few days that used to terrify you but you are not afraid of any longer?'

Joan's eyes were getting bigger and bigger as she listened.

I smiled. 'I dealt with a man who represented every thing I used to fear but no longer do.'

'Well,' Geraldine said, 'there is your answer!'

How right she was.

I had come to learn a lot about where I was in the daytime by what I dreamt. Long gone were those dreams of crawling up the chapel or of hanging on to the side of a building trying to get from one window to the next or not being able to open up my eyes because I was afraid to see what was there.

As the weeks rolled on to Christmas, Joan and I would give advice to the other women on where to go shopping across the border. Most of the woman went home for lunch and Joan and I would chat in the kitchen as we tried to stay warm or go for a walk around the town. It was funny how much she looked to England.

She didn't even know the Irish TV presenters – but then I didn't know the English ones. We decided one day that we had a lot more in common with each other than we had with either the English or the southern Irish. That is something I could never have imagined but we were both brought up in the same war.

We bonded well. Some people approached FÁS to do another course but I knew by then why I was on this course and did not need to continue with another. It would have given me the security of an income for another few months but that was not how I operated. My little voice said it was time to move on and even for money I wouldn't stay anywhere if it was time to go.

We all went out for lunch before we started our work experience. Long gone were my notions of going back to be a receptionist, even if there were any jobs, so I got work experience in a small nursing home to see if that was the direction in which I would go: running a small home for semi-independent elderly people in the house I was building. It was coming up to Christmas and I thought I'd leave all that to the New Year. I would know what to do when the time came, as I have always known.

If it feels right, do it; if it doesn't, don't: that is how I reared my children. 'Don't be listening to me or anyone else, I have no idea what your journey is but you do, so go and do it. I'll support you in whatever it is.'

Roisín had chosen Media and loved it with a passion. She had been voted best first year and best second year Media student. I was proud of her, not, as I said to her, because she was doing so well but because she had followed her dream.

Jarlath was studying Business and didn't seem to be having any problem with it. He had done very well in his first year.

They were both coming home for Christmas after their exams and Dad and Mammy were coming down as usual.

33

Moving into the Future

Dad and Mam had been coming down to me every Christmas since Marty and I separated. At first it was to support me but now I knew it was because they liked to get away. They also loved to go to Christmas Day Mass in the psychiatric home with my patients, as we had been doing for years now.

The Mass was always celebrated by Father Maloney, a lovely man in his eighties. I had known him since I first arrived. The local choir came in and afterwards everyone was served Irish coffees, cake, mince pies and all types of goodies before going home to their families. We could also visit the two patients Dad and Mam had taken care of for me so many times before they moved from my place to live in the home.

The phone rang one evening jut after I came home from class.

'I'll bring the turkey for Christmas,' said Mammy after a brief hello. 'Geraldine has made the pudding for us. The stuffing I will have made. You get the ham.'

'Great!' I said, relieved, as I would not be finishing the course until Christmas week and any help was a godsend.

'I'll get a frozen one,' she continued, 'if there are any left when I get down to Enniskillen. You know they had to close the supermarket to restock the other day. Everything was sold out. Is there no food down there at all?'

She knew quite well the difference in prices and, now with the Euro so high against sterling, people were taking full advantage of it. It was the same advantage we had all our lives. We lived on the border and we shopped on whichever side things were cheaper. I remember when we were kids there were times all the shopping was done in Clones, on the southern side of the border. Mam and Dad would go there on a Saturday night, do their shopping and then go for a drink and come home with ice lollies for all of us. Tobacco was a lot cheaper in the Republic at the time and Dad smoked a pipe. Clones was now a dead town and had been for a long time.

With that much organised I decided I would go up and take Dad and Mam to Craigavon for the day so I could get what I needed for the kids.

The people of Newry were now going to Craigavon to shop, as they could not get through their own town with the influx of southern shoppers. So I went up to Fermanagh and headed up the M1 to avoid my Roscommon neighbours in Enniskillen.

As we headed up the motorway Ruth texted me the directions for the shopping centre as Dad navigated from the back seat with a can of Guinness in his hand.

We had a great day and I came back with all the presents and extras for Christmas.

Dad and Mam loved to be driven about even though the two of them were still driving at eighty and ninety. Ruth was to come too but as Teagan would take up half the car with her bits and pieces she decided to stay at home and go with Gertie the next day.

Ruth had got pregnant in her forties when she thought she had finished her family. On a November morning Ruth paced the labour ward in Enniskillen twenty-one years and a day after Roisín had been born there. I paced the floor of the classroom in Ballagh, Geraldine the floor of her home in Antrim, Gertie hers in Cavan, Lucy hers in Florida and Mammy was up to high doh at home but Teagan was born with no problems, all six pounds one ounce of her, and was thriving.

After the work experience we all met that last morning in Ballagh and exchanged phone numbers and email addresses. Joan was going back to work in the North and Mary and I had become firm friends and would be walking together. The rest I knew I would meet occasionally but it was time to let go and move on to whatever!

Joan and I hugged and she said as she was leaving, 'I'll type that book for you when you write it.'

I laughed and went home to clean the house for everyone to arrive. The house was a mess as I had been very busy with the course, work experience and going up home and I decided to leave it all to do at one time. I loved cleaning as I found it great therapy and decided to start at the windows as they were filthy from the traffic on the road.

Down I went to my neighbour Kevin to borrow the ladder to clean them on the outside, I went in and was given the usual glass of orange juice, which he knew was all I would take.

Kevin and his kids were like an extended family to me. His wife had died in her thirties and he had reared nine children alone. His girls, Jenny, Maryanne and Olivia, had helped me to rear my pair since I moved in. They were only children themselves at the time but old enough to take Roisín and Jarlath for walks and away to their house as I tried to catch up with work. They were a blessing to me. Now, with all the girls gone, Kevin lived with two sons but was there most of the day alone and I would visit him sometimes as I came back from my walk.

In the past few years I would have told him lots about my childhood. We had become firm friends and I would borrow his ladder or tools, as I only occasionally needed them and mine were all left in Foxford now.

'Take it, take it,' he said, 'and you're very welcome to it. I'll carry it up for you.'

'You will not I!' John and I will be right back for it.'

John was my last remaining patient. I minded him and he minded me. He helped me in the garden, put out the bins, tidied up the front of the house and kept all tidy downstairs for me on a day-to-day basis. His friend Jacinta would come up every evening to have her tea with him. On Saturday and Sunday I would make dinner for them so it worked out well for all of us.

John picked up the ladder as he insisted he was fine to bring it on his own. He set it up as he always did and I started cleaning. I had all the outsides done before the rain and the ladder left back, then I started on one room at a time. I tackled the sitting room first, which was not a problem as it was never used now unless Dad and Mam were down, so it was dusted and the decorations put up, long past their date, as Christmas was only three days away.

The kitchen was next to be scrubbed that night; then I buzzed around my office and the hall press and they were soon sorted.

I went to bed, exhausted, and next morning started on my room, which looked as if a bomb had hit it. Dad and Mam slept in my room when they came down as it now had the only double bed in the house and I would sleep wherever there was a bed, usually Roisín's room – another reason I wanted to finish the new house, to have plenty of room for everyone.

For years as I lay in bed at night I would get into the habit of writing if I was having nightmares and the locker drawers were full of papers I had written on. They were usually very angry words and poems. I found it was wonderful therapy to leave my anger on paper. I sat on the bed and had started to read them when my wee voice shouted, 'Burn them, Burn them.'

I couldn't believe how loud it was but I thought, 'I can't burn them. I'll read them.'

'Burn them!' it repeated.

I left them on the bed and continued to clean and vacuum the room. I watched the papers out of the corner of my eye and thought, 'How can I burn you? You tell what I've been through and for the past seven years I cried as I wrote you, cried with the pain. Don't I need to remember? Don't I need my children to know what it was like?'

I was very confused so I went and got my coat and out the door for a walk. I usually solved these dilemmas on a walk or in my meditation. I walked and talked and listened to the same words repeat themselves. When I got back home I decided to do a meditation to the wonderful place called home and the answer there was the same I had heard all morning.

I picked up the papers and ripped them up without reading a word. I took them into the sitting room and put them in the grate and went looking for a match. I couldn't find one, nor a lighter that would work, so I left them in the grate and continued my cleaning.

When the kids arrived later that night from the two sides of the country all was cleaned and the dinner ready. After they had eaten, they went over to see their Dad next door. Next day, with Roisín and Jarlath still sleeping, I headed off to walk and when I was returning saw the smoke from the chimney and knew that Dad and Mam had arrived and all my writings were burnt.

Mam was on a mission and started making the sherry trifle and the stuffing and I was handed the list of instructions for cooking the turkey. Christ, I thought, we used to just wring its neck, plucks its feather, singe the small hairs and put it in the oven. Now you were not allowed to let it touch anything else, it could only be stuffed through the neck, it took half an hour to figure how long it was going to take to cook. But what once would have driven me nuts I could now laugh at with good humour.

Well, the frozen turkey was still not defrosted when we were going to bed. Early next morning I heard Mam up and down the corridor. 'Put that turkey on,' she said when she saw me appear.

You can't imagine how annoyed she was when the turkey still wasn't defrosted and it out of the freezer for days.

'It's okay, Mam,' I said, 'we'll take the giblets out and it will be fine for an evening dinner.'

What could she do but laugh and say, 'What will we eat between this and that?'

'I doubt if we'll go hungry!' I said.

Later as the turkey lay defrosted in the middle of the kitchen, I stuffed the little bit I was allowed to and gladly put it in the oven.

My wee voice was speaking again. It didn't even take a rest at Christmas. I listened, picked up my mobile and texted Dave: 'Thank you, Dave, for the past eight years, for your time, your love and your patience, in helping me get to this wonderful place I am in. You are a true friend.'

I sent it off and went back to cooking the dinner.

It was lovely to sit down to eat with my parents and children, but to be honest I was sick of that turkey and ate very little of it. Two days later Dad and Mam went home, knowing that Roisín and I would be up in a few days for New Year's Day.

34

TRUST YOUR GUT

Now back in my mother's kitchen on the second day of the New Year I looked up at the clock, which had moved to 2.20 in what seemed like a flash. Some of the family were still there but most had left. Ruth had slipped out quietly a few hours earlier with a tired baby to get their much-needed rest. Roisín and Sineád were still whispering and giggling in their beds, although exhausted from the Christmas festivities.

Brendan and Gertie had gone back over the border and Peter's new family to their beds across the road in Noel's house.

Mammy had left when all were fed. Her hearing was not great and she did not like crowds. Daddy followed her an hour later.

The rest of us were talking, which we were all experts at.

When she was a child, Roisín once asked me, 'Mammy, why can't I be a good at football like Jarlath?'

'Because you're like the Lynches,' I replied.

'What are they good at?'

'Talking!' I answered.

'What good is that?' she asked, disappointed.

'Roisín,' I said, 'if you can talk you can get anywhere and solve all kinds of problems.'

I don't think she understood but I knew. Here we were in a community that was seeing peace for the first time in decades, a peace that was built on talking and that had a foundation strong enough to last. It was a peace that members of this family had contributed to, as they did Trojan work (and talking) for Sinn Féin.

Eventually, the door from the hallway opened and Mammy's head appeared and she said, 'Children do you not think it's time you went to your beds?'

We all laughed together and everyone rose and went to wherever we were to sleep that night.

On 3 January Roisín and I crossed the border again, this time in daylight, heading home to the west. Exhaustion had caught up with her and we drove along in silence. There was a feeling in me that something had just completed its cycle and that some big part of my life was over.

'Is this the end?' I thought. 'Or is the beginning of something completely new?'

I had spent fifteen years now actively dealing with the effects of post-traumatic stress; the depression, the nightmares and the flashbacks of memories buried deep within my being. All I knew was that I was better. I had overed it, as they say in the North.

We stopped with Gertie, my youngest sister, so I could show Roisín her new house. Well, that wasn't my only reason.

Gertie was a yoga teacher and had helped me out a few weeks before when I hurt my back dancing all night in a pair of high shoes. That day, she had put me in the strangest position on her floor and nearly sat on me and I was straight as a die after it but now I needed another treatment. I had a pain in my right hip, from driving, I thought. Having it stretched was foremost in my mind, as I doubted if I would get home in the state I was in.

Well, if I thought I was in strange position the previous time it was nothing as strange as the one Gertie put me in that morning. Roisín looked on in amusement.

The pain shot down my leg as I stretched it but it was great, just what the doctor ordered, and I left in better shape.

Jarlath called as we were nearing home. 'Where are you now?' he said, as he always did when he called.

'Elphin. See you in half an hour.'

Better feed him tonight, I thought. I had been away for two days and was feeling a little guilty, as any good mother would. I seemed to have done nothing over Christmas but feed him and Roisín but I had thoroughly enjoyed it.

'What am I going to do now?' I thought, now that the festive season was over and the New Year had started to force thoughts of my future.

My course had just finished with FÁS and I could type twenty-five words a minute but with the recession rampant my options were lessening by the minute.

I can still see the face of the local FÁS boss that last morning in

December two weeks before, when he asked what we got out of the course.

'Well,' said I, 'honestly, I know I will never work for anyone. I have just finished up a business after twenty-one years and getting up every morning for the past seventeen weeks and being somewhere at a specific time has taught me that I have no intention of working for anybody but myself.'

'So what will you do?' he asked.

'I have no idea yet but I will work for myself and with a bit of luck I'll employ someone else to help me.'

'Well,' he said, 'that's good. You've got out of it exactly what you wanted,' and I knew he meant it.

We arrived as Jarlath was leaving. He gave me a hug and not a mention of food, thank God. The house was in a bit of a mess but not too bad after two days of neglect.

I headed to the bedroom for a quick meditation to get myself together. No more thoughts of the future as I went to that wonderful place in myself I had found in meditation, that place that had sustained me for the past twenty-five years.

On Sunday morning two friends picked me up as I was leading a walk across the bogs, fields and back roads of Roscommon. As the six of us walked across the fields, I thought, 'This is heaven.'

We walked as we always did, slipping in and out of conversations as we moved from one person to another to catch up with the new year's resolutions. I had decided to have none this year but to go with the flow, something I had been trying all my life to do. I told stories of the Troubles with a humour that had everyone in stitches laughing.

As we approached the back road into Castlerea, the town that had kept me for the past twenty-one years, I thought, 'Is it time to move on and if it is how will I manage to get the money to finish my house?' I made the dinner and went off to bed exhausted.

Unusually for me, I woke a few times that night with an unbearable pain in my hip and down my leg. 'What is leaving my body now?' was my thought as I drifted back to sleep. The hip was where I held fear.

I woke in the morning and said to the world, 'Take me where it is I am to go from here,' which was my mantra of late.

My conscious mind kept asking, 'What if you can't pay the

mortgage? What if you can't pay the college expenses? What if? What if? What if?'

'Oh shut up!' I said as I got out of bed.

I had been here many times before and I knew that money was the least of my problems.

I walked into the kitchen and turned on the radio to drown the thoughts and avoid the phone calls I needed to make.

'I'll listen to Gerry Ryan, he'll cheer me up,' I thought, but he was not presenting the show so I reached to switch it off.

As I did, a woman said, 'If you ever thought you could write a book stay tuned, as I have one of Ireland's top writers here to tell you how to get started.'

'You should write a book, you should write a book.' If I was paid every time someone had that said to me I would not need to work.

Two thousand words a chapter, a hundred thousand words for a book, were the only two things I wrote on a piece of paper.

I figured that counted me out. Who could possibly write that much? I had never written more than a few pages at any one time.

'It took me six weeks to write the first two thousand words,' the woman said next.

The wee voice in my head said, 'Just sit down and see what happens.' I turned off the radio and switched on the computer and started typing.

Did I say I could type twenty-five words a minute? Well, two hours later, still in my pyjamas, I had written two thousand words and my only thought was, 'Thank God for word count!'

Just after I finished writing this book two soldiers were shot in Antrim on a Saturday night and a policeman the following Monday night. I could not watch it on the news but everyone asked me, 'Will it start again?'

'I don't know,' I replied, 'but I don't think so. We could never go back there.'

My sister told me that the police were back on the streets carrying their big guns. I went to bed uneasy and dreamed that I was trying to wake up but I could not open my eyes or move my body. It was a while since I had this nightmare.

I woke up and stared at the ceiling for a long time, knowing that I would have to go into a meditation to figure out what was wrong. I didn't want to know but I had to know or I would not be able to cope, waiting for the nightmare to return when I tried to sleep.

I sat up in my bed and went back into the dream and I started to shake. My jaw was moving so fast that my teeth were chattering, like I was frozen. It sounded like a machine gun. I cried and I had a flashback. I was back in that cell, sitting at one side of a table with a policeman and woman at the other side and someone behind me. In the middle of the table was a revolver, which they had emptied, and they put one bullet back in it, in front of me. They told me it would take only one to blow my brains out.

My body shook as I tried to breathe in my bed, over thirty years later. My body is still shaking as I write this. That gun lay there for the duration of the interview and was lifted only when they took it and put it to my head and repeated, 'Who the fuck would miss you anyway? There are far too many of you bastards. I'm quite sure your mother would be glad to be rid of you.'

Andy was right: these things do not go away. We have to learn to live with the brutality that comes with being in a war.

Epilogue

The freedom to set off on my own journey brought me face-to-face with some terrible demons. Even though I now knew the truth, the fear was still there.

That day in May 2009, after emailing my editor, Eileen, I was going to the mountains to help a friend to lead a walk for an annual walking festival. We had a wonderful day and I came back feeling great but as soon as I got home I was crying again. That terrible fear was back.

I could not get into a meditation but curled in a ball and watched television, oblivious to what was on it or what was going on in me.

I read as I always did in bed but as I was going to sleep I felt a presence in the room, that of a trusted friend who I knew would protect me as I cried myself to sleep. I woke in the early morning with a tightness in my chest that rose to my throat and that I thought would choke me.

When I was able I sent this message:

> Hi Eileen
> A few other things I have realised since I last emailed you and why a poem I wrote a few years ago makes so much sense now:
>
> *Another Time*
>
> *How many times have I gone back,*
> *Back to my past,*
> *And picked you up there, Mary, and taken you into my soul,*
> *For warmth,*
> *For love,*
> *For healing?*

You who had been frozen in time, in a memory,
Locked so deep, no body could have found you but me,
I was just waiting, waiting until I was strong enough,
To unlock that door and take you home to heal.
Forgive me for taking so long,
But I had the madness, the silliness of life to distract me.
Until you screamed so loud, I had no choice but to listen,
And I am so very glad I did,
And loved you back into my life and know I was blessed to have
*   found another part of me and welcomed her home,*
And then,
When I thought I had picked up all the pieces to make me whole
*   again,*
You would cry from another place, another time,
Some times you would have to scream through my dreams
*   because I thought we were complete,*
But again I would go back through my meditation and take you
*   into my soul,*
For shelter and healing,
And I thank God for another piece of my jigsaw that unravels
*   the confusion of my life.*

Yesterday when I went into my meditation I was
back in the car heading for the checkpoint. I stopped
the car and took her out (I don't set out to bring these
things into my meditations; mostly they automatically
come about). She was petrified. I took her into my
wee room and put her to bed. She was a dead weight
from exhaustion and fear. Of course I tried to talk to
her but she never opened her mouth, just lay there in a
ball, staring into space. I wrapped her in a pink fleece
blanket and sat with her for a short while, as I knew she
did not want me near her. When I went back into my
meditation last night she had not budged one inch. She
was still just lying there staring.

This morning I realised a few other things that were
probably obvious to others to whom I have told this
story to but not to me.

The first is something I only realised this year; the

police held me illegally. They would have needed to arrest me to have held me that long and they didn't arrest me. If I had admitted this to myself at the time I would have had to do something about it.

If I had told anyone I would have had a case against them. Now, Eileen, in the 1970s a case against the police was possible but not advisable for a number of reasons.

They would harass you and your family constantly. (That was already happening but it could definitely have been worse. I would have had no choice but to leave anyway and I would not have been able to go home ever, even to visit.)

They would have lied through their teeth as they always did and they had the law behind them, even though they had broken it.

I have no doubt there would have been retaliation and I did not want that on my head and I would still never been able to cross the border.

If there was retaliation I would be in a position where I automatically became part of something that I understood but had no intention of joining. I knew this from my response when I was asked to bring that bomb into the hotel, even though I was aware at the age of twelve that I could and would kill, but only in self-defence.

Talk soon

Mary

Feeling a lot better I set out to pick Roisín up from college. The day was another glorious one and I sang at the top of my voice to Kris Kristofferson's *Greatest Hits*. I had bought the CD in Galway a few weeks before and had not listened to anything else since. As I continued to drive and sing I realised this was not ordinary singing; this was coming from the pit of my stomach. I remembered that I had this album as a teenager and had broken it from overuse.

Somewhere between Roscommon and Athlone the singing turned to screams and I had to pull in to the side of the road to find tissues. I was now crying so much I needed time to release it.

I knew instantly that these screams and tears were those of an eighteen-year-old who had never been allowed to express herself before.

When it was over I continued my journey. I was no longer able to sing but I was very aware of what had happened; the girl in my wee room had let go and released the fear in her, the fear she had had in that car at that checkpoint for nearly thirty-two years.

When we reached home later that afternoon I checked my emails and there was one back from Eileen who said:

> Hi Mary
>
> I think you're an incredibly brave woman to be dealing with all this so well!!
>
> I have learned to trust my intuition and not to look for logic in what it's telling me to do! Right now, it's telling me to remind you that everybody does the best they can in any situation with the level of consciousness they've reached.
>
> You were doing your best at every turn – but so were the people who tortured you in so many ways.
>
> If it were possible to go back as you are now to those times, you would react differently because you have now reached a higher level of consciousness. There is no need to regret anything. You did your best and that is all anybody can do.
>
> I understand the fear.
>
> Acknowledge it, feel it, thank it for the role it played in keeping you safe in dangerous situations and then kiss it goodbye! You don't need it any more.
>
> This book will help to release so many people who are imprisoned by their past pain. Your life will serve as a road map for others – that's a rare privilege!
>
> Talk soon
>
> Eileen x

I left Roisín resting and I headed out for my walk, wanting to be alone with my thoughts. I thought a lot about what Eileen had said and the fact that she understood what I was expressing – but why else would the world have sent her to me to edit my book?

She had said I needed to thank the fear and let it go and how right she was.

I was letting it go but I had forgotten to thank it for all those years it protected me from telling this story, thus protecting me from myself and my own doubt about what really happened to me and why I could not tell.

I thanked it from the bottom of my heart as I sat in the shade of my favourite tree. I let it go and explained to it that I was strong enough to face this and that I believed I would be given all the help I needed to move on.

Later in my meditation I sat with my younger self in front of me on my knees, the pink fleece blanket over us both as we got to know and trust each other, even though not a word was spoken between us.

Before going to bed I emailed Eileen again:

> Hi Eileen
>
> Thanks for the reminder as I was letting it go but I had forgotten to thank it for the part it had played in protecting me. I really do not need it any more, and as I drove to Maynooth today to pick up Roisín I felt it leave my body and it was painful.
>
> Funny thing, Eileen, is that if I were to go back I doubt if I would change anything. This was all part of my journey and I understand it now. I will say it would have been much easier if I had told someone a long time ago but it was not to be.
>
> Love
>
> Mary

Next mornin, in my meditation I told my younger self exactly what I told Eileen the night before: if I were to go back to that time again I would not change anything as there were no other options. I thanked her for doing the right thing and told her that I was so proud of her for being so wise at such a young age.

Later in the day when I spoke to my sister Geraldine and read what I had written she said, 'I understand that so well, Mary. I would have done the very same thing. How could you have told

Mammy? She had more than enough to cope with. We all coped with our own stuff.'

I let it go at the speed I could cope with. When it has gone the part of me that I left in that car so long ago – that strong, brave, wise girl – will be a part of my everyday life and such a benefit to my whole future.

Face your fear, thank it and let it go. Allow another part of you home to make you more complete and in less need of reaching out to others for things that are abundant in yourself.

Moving On

Move on,
Move on with your learning,
Let go,
Let go of those you have learned from.
Grow,
Grow in what you have learned.
Thank,
Thank all who have taught you, no matter how harshly.
Love,
Most of all love them,
Unconditionally,
And let them go.
This was all part of your journey,
They were there to teach you.

This poem was written about Roisín's cat, Lily, after the book was completed:

Perfect Strangers

We've met in the doorway for nearly five years now,
You and I, perfect strangers.

You barely acknowledged my presence, nor I yours.

It was not of my choosing that you came to live with us,
But of a teenager, lost after the death of her dog.

When she moved on, you could not.
You were left with no choice but to stay behind.
I continued to feed you and ignore you, as you did me.

Today as I sat in the sun eating my breakfast at two,
You came to me,
Graceful, playful and friendly, like never before.
Was everything so obvious to you?
The change in me.
The frame that no longer carried thirty years of war and secrets.
Outed in a book that few may ever read.
But in a book that now contains them, no longer in the cells of
    my being.

I stroked your shiny coat, and you let me.

A Note from the Author

I now run a meditation, walking and writing centre in Foxford, County Mayo, where you can learn to use the techniques I have described in this book and others to help you to find your inner voice, your true self and your way home. Should you wish to reach me you can contact me at mary@marylynch.ie or check out my website: www.marylynch.ie.

Thank you for taking the time to read my story.

Love and best wishes always

Mary